TEACHING
the
FEMALE
Brain

*In memory of the wonderful women
who opened the worlds of
science and math
to many students (including the author):*

*Nancy Lee Young
Jessie Y. Carpenter Goulding*

TEACHING the FEMALE Brain

How Girls Learn Math and Science

Abigail Norfleet James

CORWIN
A SAGE Company

For information:

Corwin
A SAGE Company
2455 Teller Road
Thousand Oaks, California 91320
(800) 233-9936
Fax: (800) 417-2466
www.corwinpress.com

SAGE India Pvt. Ltd.
B 1/I 1 Mohan Cooperative
    Industrial Area
Mathura Road, New Delhi 110 044
India

SAGE Ltd.
1 Oliver's Yard
55 City Road
London EC1Y 1SP
United Kingdom

SAGE Asia-Pacific Pte. Ltd.
33 Pekin Street #02-01
Far East Square
Singapore 048763

Printed in the United States of America.

Library of Congress Cataloging-in-Publication Data

James, Abigail Norfleet.
Teaching the female brain : How girls learn math and science / Abigail Norfleet James.
        p. cm.
Includes bibliographical references and index.
ISBN 978-1-4129-6709-9 (cloth)
ISBN 978-1-4129-6710-5 (pbk.)
    1. Mathematics—Study and teaching.   2. Science—Study and teaching.   3. Girls—Education.   4. Girls—Psychology.   5. Sex differences in education.   I. Title.

QA11.2.J36 2009
510.71—dc22   2009010945

This book is printed on acid-free paper.

09   10   11   12   13   10   9   8   7   6   5   4   3   2   1

Acquisitions Editor:	Carol Chambers Collins
Editorial Assistant:	Brett Ory
Production Editor:	Eric Garner
Copy Editor:	Codi Bowman
Typesetter:	C&M Digitals (P) Ltd.
Proofreader:	Susan Schon
Indexer:	Terri Corry
Cover Designer:	Karine Hovsepian

Contents

Foreword

In the spring, when schedules are set for the following school year, I am never surprised when a handful of girls line up at the head of upper school's office door. These students are concerned because calculus, advanced-placement (AP) physics, or AP chemistry appears on their class schedules. They are sure that someone has made a mistake. Despite many years spent in a single-sex school that actively promotes girls' achievements in the disciplines of science, technology, engineering, and math (STEM), many girls still doubt their ability to excel in these academic areas.

Why does this happen year after year? How can these girls develop confidence in their ability? Why does this anxiety affect some girls and not others? What is the difference between test anxiety and math anxiety? Educators and parents have spent years searching for answers.

Fortunately, researchers have some answers and are working toward many more. An ever-increasing body of research is enhancing our knowledge about the complex relationship between gender and cognition. Researchers have focused on the similar and different ways girls' and boys' brains process information.

Their findings, though varied in scope, support the conclusion that girls' brains differ in several key ways from boys' brains and that the resulting differences influence how girls and boys learn. Most recently, scientific research has expanded to include the use of magnetic resonance imaging (MRI) to understand better neurological growth and connections. Additionally, studies in educational psychology and sociology continue to make important contributions to this field of research. With this expanding body of knowledge, synthesis and real-world application are needed to realize its benefits.

Teaching the Female Brain serves these purposes and builds on the key concepts established in Dr. Abigail Norfleet James's first book, *Teaching the Male Brain* (2007), which outlines the cognitive, sensory, physical, social, and emotional differences between genders. Following each area of her synthesis of the latest research, overview of brain functions, and explanation of learning modalities—which includes learning differences—Dr. James provides many practical strategies for using this information. Her chapter on stress, test anxiety, math anxiety, and the typically overlooked topic of self-handicapping is particularly helpful not only to teachers but also to parents and students. Her real-world examples are insightful and will resonate with all her readers.

Taking the position that both biology and environment influence how girls learn, Dr. James focuses on making sure that teachers recognize and understand the cognitive gender differences and social influences that affect how girls learn. As teachers, parents, policymakers, and students themselves become aware of these differences and develop strategies to accommodate all students, the likelihood that girls *and* boys will have more positive learning experiences is greatly enhanced.

A psychologist and an experienced math and science teacher with years of service in all-girls', all-boys', and coeducational classrooms, Dr. James delivers practical strategies for every teacher and parent, providing age-appropriate activities and exercises. These accommodations have the potential to change the framework for educating girls in the classroom and at the school, county, and state levels.

It is a critical time for girls; the numbers of women in the STEM areas are increasing only gradually—and even declining, in terms of the number of women who earn undergraduate degrees in mathematics and computer and information science. *Teaching the Female Brain* is an invaluable resource for parents, teachers, educational policymakers, and other adults who work closely with young women and men.

Dr. James establishes a broad understanding of gender differences and an awareness of the many ways to influence positively girls' confidence in math and science. This self-assurance is essential to the success of girls in our modern, technological world as well as to their overall ability to reach their potential and to contribute to our collective future: a future where all girls embrace science, technology, engineering, and technology with enthusiasm and confidence.

—Monica M. Gillespie, PhD

Monica M. Gillespie, Head of School of St. Paul's School for Girls, holds BA, MEd, and PhD degrees from the University of Virginia. She is a former visiting-assistant professor at the Jepson School of Leadership Studies at the University of Richmond, a former assistant professor at the Curry School of Education at the University of Virginia, and an author and coauthor of research papers and articles on women in leadership and educational design.

Acknowledgments

A number of people are responsible for what is in this book. As I have grown as a teacher, I realized that I would not have become a science and math teacher if it were not for the two teachers to whom the book is dedicated. They were my middle school teachers, and I can remember both of them as if I had been in their classes yesterday. In the almost fifty years since then, few teachers have made as strong an impression on me. Role models are very important for girls, and these two women provided me with stellar examples of what scientists and mathematicians could look like.

You may have read an earlier book I wrote about teaching the male brain. Many of my acquaintances are surprised that I have taught girls as well. Roberta C. McBride gave me my first teaching job, which was at an all-girls' school. I will never forget the call from her about a week before the start of school asking me if I would mind teaching a math class along with the science classes that I was contracted for. I assumed that I would be teaching pre-algebra or Algebra I at the most only to discover that I was assigned a class of Algebra II/trigonometry students. It quickly became apparent that everyone in the class was terrified of math and was only there because they all needed a third credit in math to get into competitive universities. A true baptism by fire, but those girls made the most amazing progress, and as I wrote this book, I tried to put myself in those two classes to try to remember what it was we did. Later, I taught science and math at a different girls' school, and I thank Patrick F. Bassett for making me accept the position. I wasn't sure that I could do it, but those experiences, together with those from my earlier school, laid the groundwork for what you will find in the following pages.

After I obtained my doctorate, I took an adjunct position with Germanna Community College where I came across David Fama, who taught math. David and I had many discussions about the material in my first book about teaching boys before remarking that his problem was with his female students, not his male students. I agreed that was probably so, but what I knew about gender differences would help his students as well. Those discussions were so interesting to both of us and helped me realize that I actually knew quite a bit about how girls learn. David was responsible for arranging for me to speak at the Virginia Mathematical Association of Two-Year Colleges (VaMATYC) annual meeting. That talk was so well received, resulting in several other organizations asking for similar material, that I realized that there probably was a book in it. Without David's probing questions, I might not have gotten this information formatted as clearly.

I thank David McCrae and Ben Hale who allowed me to teach developmental math in summer school at Woodberry Forest. True, Woodberry is a boys' school, but the summer sessions included girls, and while almost all of my summer students were boys, the girls I taught helped me see what had been missing in their past math and science training. Some of the strategies that are included in this book were tried out then.

Lori Howard has been my true friend by pointing out to me where I was going seriously astray in this manuscript and helping me figure out what I actually wanted to say. She is one of the world's great teachers, and I am lucky to have had her willing help.

Others who have helped along the way are Sandra Allison, Samuels Real Estate, Robert and Catherine Gillespie, Monica M. Gillespie, Cathe Kervan, Duane Berger, St. Catherine's School, and all the schools who asked me to speak about teaching girls. Carol Collins has let me bend her ear and then set me gently on the correct path—what a good editor should do. She, her assistant Brett Ory, and Corwin have supported me in this endeavor.

My family continues to be the best of all. My son is so pleased that he supplied only one example in this book after having served as the chief example in the boy book. My husband, my best friend of all, has taken to finding me books on the brain that I would never have found, so he is now a research assistant as well as the nicest man in the world.

Corwin thanks the following reviewers for their contribution to this book.

Barbara Dullaghan
Elementary Gifted and
   Talented Specialist
Bloomington Public Schools
Bloomington, MN

Roberta E. Glaser
Retired Assistant
   Superintendent
St. Johns Public Schools
St. Johns, MI

Dolores Hennessy
Reading Specialist
Teacher
New Milford, CT

Denise Metiva Hernandez
NBCT, Educator
Pontchartrain Elementary
   School
Mandeville, LA

Toni Jones
Principal
Chula Vista Elementary School
   District
Chula Vista, CA

About the Author

 **Abigail Norfleet James** taught for many years in single-sex schools and consults on the subject of gendered teaching to school systems, colleges, and universities. Her area of expertise is developmental and educational psychology as applied to the gendered classroom. Prior to obtaining her doctorate from the University of Virginia, Curry School of Education, she taught science, biology, and psychology in both boys' and girls' secondary schools.

Previous publications include reports of research comparing the educational attitudes of male graduates of coed schools to male graduates of single-sex schools and research describing the effects of gendered basic-skills instruction. In addition, she has written on differentiated instruction at the elementary school level and on using cognitive gender differences to teach boys. She has presented workshops and papers at many educational conferences and works with teachers and parent groups in interpreting the world of gendered education.

Her professional affiliations include the American Educational Research Association, the American Psychological Association, the Association for Supervision and Curriculum Development, the Gender and Education Association, the International Boys' School Coalition, and the National Association for Single-Sex Public Education (advisory board member).

Introduction

SOURCE: Photographer: Duane Berger. Used with permission.

At the end of my junior year in high school, I had a conversation with my counselor about what I was going to take in my senior year. The year before, the girls' school that I attended had made an arrangement with the nearby boys' school to allow students at each school to attend the other school if their own school did not offer a course they wanted. I was excited as it meant that, in my senior year, I would be able to take upper-level math and science courses not available at my school. When I raised this possibility with my guidance counselor, she patted my hand and said, and I remember her words exactly, "My dear, what possible use are you *ever* going to have for calculus and physics?" I was upset, but without anyone to contradict her, I accepted her decision and took analytical algebra and biology at my own school instead.

In retrospect, I do see her point of view. After all, at that point in my life, I had decided to attend nursing school, and if that is all that I had ever done, she might have been right. However, given the changes in the profession of nursing since that time, especially with the advent of nurse practitioners, I would have had plenty of use for advanced math and science.

In the years since that time, I became a teacher of math and science and had to take calculus and physics in college, not an easy task since all of my classmates had taken the courses first in high school. I taught math and science in girls' schools and pressed each of those institutions to offer upper-level courses even if there were only a few students who expressed an interest. I was delighted to see my students enjoying these subjects and was thrilled when some of my students majored in science and math in college.

When I was in high school, it was accepted that math and science were not subjects in which most girls were going to do well. Since that time, the world has changed its perspective and now the idea is that girls should have the chance to do math and science if they want to. However, from working with young women, I have noticed that many girls believe they are probably not going to do well in math or science or, at the very least, will not be interested in those subjects, and it appears that this belief is pervasive and widespread.

Is there any evidence that math and science are not subjects for girls? See if you know the answers to the following questions.

Hint: All the individuals are women.

QUIZ

1. Who was the first person to win two Nobel Prizes?

2. Who was the first child of a Nobel Prize winner to also win a Nobel not shared with the parent?

3. Who was the inventor of the computer language COBOL?

4. Who developed the first major drug treatment for leukemia?

5. Who invented Kevlar, the material used in bulletproof vests?

6. Who led the team that developed the Mars Pathfinder rover?

7. Who invented the computer games King's Quest, The Dark Crystal, The Dagger of Amon-Ra, and Phantasmagoria?

8. Who discovered the physical basis for DNA as well as the structure of the tobacco mosaic virus?

9. Who developed the technique of radioimmunoassay, one of the most significant methods of chemical analysis used in medicine?

10. Who invented the disposable cell phone?

Answers are found on page 7.

Lest you think that these women were spending their lives in a laboratory somewhere not having a real life, six of the ten were married and they had eight children among them. More importantly, these accomplished women and many more like them did not believe that the areas of science, technology, engineering, and math (STEM) were subjects for which they were not suited. Also noteworthy is that a great many prominent women scientists and mathematicians, including some of those mentioned in the quiz, began their careers in the nineteenth or at the beginning of the twentieth century. After the beginning of the twentieth century, the number of women active in science and math dropped and has only recently shown an upturn.

Today many people are not aware that during the latter part of the nineteenth century the prevailing wisdom was that literature and classics were subjects best suited for men; women should study science and math because those subjects were practical and provided discipline and training (Tolley, 2003). In California in 1895, there were 14% more boys than girls enrolled in trigonometry and 2% more boys than girls enrolled in physics. A mere twenty years later in 1915, there were 34% more boys than girls enrolled in trigonometry and 20% more boys than girls enrolled in physics (Tyack & Hansot, 1990). While the reasons for this shift are complicated, two possible explanations for this change stand out.

The first reason has to do with access. In the nineteenth century, admission to the elite male universities required knowledge of the classics, and men who wished to attend those institutions were expected to study Greek, Latin, philosophy, and literature. It was rare for a woman to go to college, so women were encouraged to study subjects in high school that provided practical applications, specifically science. The second reason is economic. Before 1900, there were few highly remunerative careers that benefited from scientific or mathematical skills (Tolley, 2003). Once the knowledge of science began to result in highly paid jobs, men began to turn their attention to those subjects once considered better suited for women.

Even though girls were not expected to go to college at the beginning of the twentieth century, girls and boys in public high schools took basically the same academic courses. The only difference was that some girls might have taken home economics while some boys might have enrolled in manual training or vocational courses. The students may have been taking the same courses, but the assumption was that boys should have been the superior students. Reports from the era note that educators were surprised that the girls did as well if not better than the boys in most classes including mathematics (Tyack & Hansot, 1990). One suggestion made at the time for this disparity was that the more capable boys had left to seek employment. That would make the unlikely assumption that the best male students were not planning to attend a university. For whatever reason, in most courses, on average the girls' performance on exams surpassed the boys'.

The fact that boys did not do as well as girls in math was not considered a major problem because history and languages were seen as more important for higher-status jobs in offices and management. Even though they had the math and science training, women had been excluded from higher-level engineering and business positions where they might have competed with men (Posadas, 1997). By the 1930s, because of the increase in technology in business, science and math were seen to be very important for career advancement, so the percentage of men taking those courses increased and the percentage of women decreased.

When the men went off to World War II, women quickly moved into industrial management and other high-paying areas (Coleman, 2000; Posadas, 1997). Once the men came back from war, women were relegated to the lower-paying positions where educational training was not required but which were now being unionized. During the 1950s, women began to rise up the ladder in union and industrial jobs, one of many factors causing social pressure resulting in the women's movement of the 1960s and 1970s (Coleman, 2000). As women became more politically active, it was quickly apparent that the abysmal state of math and science training for women was preventing them from obtaining employment in highly paid technical fields. In fact, between the 1900s when math and science were considered women's courses and the 1960s, the idea had developed that math and science were not subjects in which girls could do well (American Association of University Women [AAUW], 1992). One facet of the women's movement has been on helping girls obtain parity in education, especially in technical fields.

The rebound of women in science and math is beginning. In 1978, 11% of bachelor's degrees in physics were awarded to women; by 2004, women received 23% of bachelor's degrees in physics. Doctorate degrees for women in the same field are showing a similar upturn from 7% in 1978 to 16% in 2004 (Mulvey & Nicholson, 2006). Astronomy was considered part of natural history and, therefore, during the late nineteenth century, studied by more girls than boys (Tolley, 2003). In 1978, only 14% of all bachelor's degrees in astronomy were awarded to women, but by 2004, women received 38% of those degrees (Mulvey & Nicholson, 2006).

Great strides for women have been made in the STEM areas. As you can see from Table 0.1, women are graduating with degrees in these areas in increasing proportions even though the total number of students in math, physics, and engineering has dropped. Only the areas of biological and computer sciences have shown consistent growth in the total numbers of students graduating with degrees in those areas.

Table 0.1   Percentage of Degrees Presented to Women in Various Academic Disciplines: Comparing Data From Previous and Recent Years

	Bachelor Degrees	Bachelor Degrees in 2006	Doctorate Degrees	Doctorate Degrees in 2006
Math and statistics	(1950) 22%	45%	(1950) 5.6%	29.5%
Biological and biomedical sciences	(1952) 26%	62%	(1952) 11%	49%
Computer and information science	(1971) 13.5%	20.6%	(1971) 2%	22%
Engineering and engineering technologies	(1950) 0.3%	17.9%	(1950) 0.2%	20%
Physical sciences and science technologies	(1960) 12.5%	42%	(1960) 3%	30%

SOURCE: U.S. Department of Education, National Center for Education Statistics, 2007 (http://nces .ed.gov/programs/digest/d07/tables_3.asp)

Engineering has worked hard to attract women, and the numbers of women entering that field do show consistent gains. Recently, women's colleges have begun to provide programs to help women enter the various engineering fields. You will find a list some of these various projects and programs in Chapter 8.

Other careers requiring knowledge of science or math are showing an increase in the numbers of women. A majority of financial specialists (54%) and those in health-diagnosing fields (70%) are women. On the other hand, the numbers of women in computer and mathematical occupations are small (30%), and those in architecture and engineering occupations even smaller (13.5%) (U.S. Census Bureau, 2000).

THE PROBLEM

The improvement that women have made in their representation in science and math is well noted, but the progress is slow. The recent position paper from the AAUW (2008) on STEM education makes it clear that even though girls are making great strides in these areas, they still have a lot of ground to make up. An important point made by the AAUW is that if women joined the technological fields in the same proportion as they are represented in the labor force as a whole, the job shortages that presently exist in the STEM areas would disappear.

Additionally, the numbers of women in some areas are beginning to drop again. In 2001, the percentage of bachelor degrees awarded to women in mathematics and statistics was 48%, and in 2006, women obtained 45% of those degrees. In 2001, the percentage of bachelor degrees awarded to women in computer and information science was 27.2%, and in 2006, that number had dropped to 20.6% (U.S. Department of Education, National Center for Education Statistics, 2007). The downward trend in these two areas is a concern to those who hope to interest girls in STEM careers.

The reasons for the slow inclusion of women into technical fields are complex. For the teacher, however, the only concern should be in making sure that all students, girls included, receive the best education possible. What that means is that the exploration of different strategies and approaches to teaching science and math will widen the range of learning opportunities benefiting each student in the classroom.

HOW TO HELP

There are substantial cognitive gender differences that can make a major impact on how girls and boys experience the classroom. Chapter 1 will cover those differences and will suggest ways for you to help girls learn by altering the presentation of material to suit the ways they best process information. Specific strategies for math (Chapter 4) and science (Chapter 5) will be covered in this book. The recommended approaches will be predicated on cognitive-gender differences and learning-style differences and will provide explicit methods for each subject.

You will notice that the title of this book is about the female brain and not about teaching math and science to girls. The problems that some girls have with STEM courses have two origins. The first is social pressure to conform to the stereotype that many girls cannot do well in math and science. Some of the suggestions that you will find in this book are designed to help your students change their opinions about what courses are suitable for girls. The second is connected with differences in learning styles, which can have an effect on the way students acquire information. You will find some boys who approach the learning process in ways similar to girls, and they will also benefit from approaches discussed here.

Finally, suggestions for developing schoolwide programs to help all students will be covered. The numbers of students enrolled in math and science courses have dropped for both boys and girls, and encouraging participation in programs in STEM topics will help all students.

Remember, not all girls will approach math and science in the same way, and you will find some boys who learn these subjects more like most of the girls. It is very important that you and your students understand that these suggestions will help all students, including some who do well in math and science.

ANSWERS TO QUIZ

1. Marie Curie for physics and chemistry—in fact, she is the *only* person to win two Nobel Prizes in two *different* sciences

2. Irene Joliot-Curie for chemistry

3. Admiral Grace Murray Hopper

4. Gertrude Belle Elion

5. Stephanie L. Kwolek

6. Donna Shirley

7. Roberta Williams

8. Rosalind Franklin—could not share in the Nobel Prize awarded to Watson and Crick because she died of cancer before the prize was awarded and the Nobel is not awarded posthumously

9. Rosalyn S. Yalow—for which she was awarded the Nobel Prize in physiology or medicine in 1977

10. Randice-Lisa Atschul—okay, so that didn't surprise you!

1

The Influence of Cognitive Gender Differences

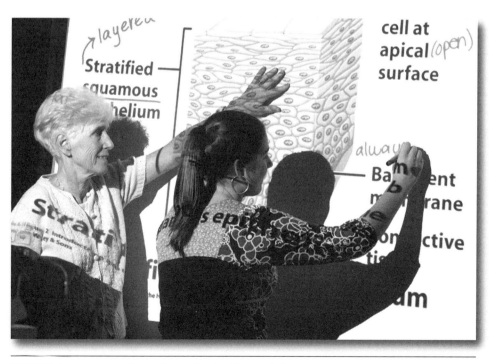

SOURCE: Photographer: Duane Berger. Used with permission.

When I proposed to write a book about the strategies I have used and my experiences in teaching math and science to girls, I received two responses from women. One group asked me if such a book is actually needed as girls are doing so much better in the technical areas. The other group said something like, "That's great. I wish I had had that when I was in school, and I know many girls who can use some help now."

Many people, both women and men, have expressed the belief that the way women think is not conducive to doing well in math even though, as you have seen from the previous chapter, women have done very well in science, technology, engineering, and math (STEM) careers. What do we know about cognitive gender differences with respect to how we learn math and science, and do those differences account for the problems that some girls seem to have in math? How extreme are the cognitive gender differences present in very young children?

QUIZ

Respond to the following statements about cognitive abilities by indicating whether the statement best describes (a) girls, (b) boys, or (c) both girls and boys.

1. Hear quieter and higher-pitched sounds better

2. Are more comfortable when the room is colder

3. Are more active

4. Can focus on moving objects better at one year of age

5. Have more connections between neurons in the brain

6. The left side of their brain matures sooner

7. Can throw objects at a target better at an earlier age

8. Have a higher tolerance for pain

9. Are more likely to use a visual strategy to remember something

10. Are more likely to use concrete methods to solve arithmetic problems

Answers are on page 31.

What we know about cognitive gender differences and the applications of this knowledge to the classroom is fairly new. What follows is an account of the latest research about gender differences in the brain and cognition, which has implications for those who are interested in maximizing the potential of the female brain in the math and science classroom.

I will try to make this brief, but this will provide a basis for future discussions about learning strategies. Using this information will help you tailor your teaching so that all students have a chance to learn in the way that best suits them. Please remember that what follows refers to average differences and individuals may only exhibit some of the features.

In the recent past, the differences between genders were usually ascribed to social construction, the belief that children learn how to behave as girls and boys by observing adults, usually their parents, or by being taught what was appropriate (Witt, 1997). With new visualizing techniques, we are beginning to be able to observe what parts of the brain are functioning when an individual is involved with a task, and we note that, in some respects, males and females do not process information in similar ways. This indicates that what women and men think and how they behave may be more influenced by the brain than previously thought. The more important point is that the differences are present very early (Giedd, Blumenthal, Jeffries, Castellanos, et al., 1999), in some cases at birth (Connellan, Baron-Cohen, Wheelwright, Batki, & Ahluwalia, 2000), indicating the early influence of biology. How much gender roles are influenced by biology and how much by environment is still a matter of conjecture, but it is evident that both influences are involved. With the new information about cognitive differences, we need to let girls know that they are not limited by biology and that there are many reasons why they can do well in math and science. All they need are strategies and confidence, and you can help them acquire both.

If girls and boys are not processing information in the same way, this has implications for the classroom. Teachers need to be cognizant of these differences and understand that not only do children learn differently but also good students may learn differently from the way the teacher learns. If a child approaches a learning task in a way that is different from the way the teacher would, that does not necessarily make either approach better or worse than the other, just different.

I believe strongly that using this information will help all of your students. However, there are two sides to the academic arguments about cognitive gender differences. One group looks at research on adults and concludes that because men and women don't differ a great deal on cognitive measures, education of children should focus on the similarities that exist between girls and boys. Generally, this group believes that if gendered educational principles are used, the differences between boys and girls will widen. The other group looks at research on the many cognitive gender differences present at birth and in young children. The conclusion drawn by this group is that the problems that girls have with math and science and that boys have with language arts begin early and only by using gendered educational approaches will men and women become more equal in their cognitive abilities. Just so you know, there is no research that has found definitive proof one way or the other.

PART 1: THE BRAIN AND SENSES

There is a big difference between the brain and the mind. The brain is the organ that sits inside our skull, and there is a great deal of controversy over how much influence the structure of your brain has on your thinking and reasoning abilities—your mind. With modern imaging techniques, scientists are looking closely to see what parts of the brain respond when an individual is directed to think certain thoughts. Consequently, we now know the location in the brain for some mental functions. However, what we know is similar to knowing that a key, electricity, and a starter motor are needed to start the engine in a car. Knowing what structures are involved does not help us understand the process, and that is what scientists are still looking for. What we do know is interesting, but the question remains: How are differences in brain development and function reflected by the differences in cognition?

Any discussion about the cognitive differences between the typical male brain and the typical female brain must accept that, on average, boys and girls differ, but that difference is not absolute. For example, I am tall for a woman, 5 feet 10 inches, which is the average height of a man in the United States. That does not make me a man; it just means I am a tall woman. Even though the average differences between girls and boys are small, there is a consistent and predictable difference. Consequently, many of your female students will benefit from the suggested teaching and learning strategies contained here, but not all. On the other hand, a few of the students who will benefit will be male.

What the Brain Looks Like

In discussing their abilities in math and science, one of the most common statements that many women make is that they can't do those subjects because they are not left-brained. The cerebrum, the largest part of the brain, is composed of two similar, but not identical halves, and the popular notion is that the left side of the brain performs logical tasks and the right side of the brain uses intuition to process information. Each half of the cerebrum is composed of four similar, but not identical, lobes that do different tasks.

The Lobes of the Cerebrum

The frontal lobe is located at the front of the brain and is involved in decision making, impulse control, and working memory. We now know that this portion of the brain develops slowly and is the last to complete development. On average, the female frontal lobes are completely developed by ages 16 to 20, whereas the male frontal lobes may not develop completely until age 25 (De Bellis et al., 2001; Giedd, Blumenthal, Jeffries, Castellanos, et al., 1999; Njemanze, 2007).

The occipital lobe is located at the very back of the brain and is involved in helping us translate the neural impulses from our eyes into the sensation we call vision. The left occipital lobe receives information primarily from the right eye, and the right lobe gets information primarily from the left eye. It takes both halves of our occipital lobe receiving information from both eyes to enable us to see in three dimensions.

The parietal lobe is located between the frontal lobe and the occipital lobe at the top of the head. Part of this lobe is involved in receiving and understanding sensations from the body. The section of the parietal lobe that is responsible for perceiving sensation is next to the frontal lobe at the top of the head. Another part of this lobe appears to be involved in combining those sensations to allow us to manage spatial information as well as helping with memory.

The temporal lobe is located above the ears on both sides of the brain. Because of the location of this lobe, it makes sense that it is involved in hearing. Another important function of the left temporal lobe is in developing language skills, although research indicates that females may use some of the right temporal lobe to do this as well (Shaywitz et al., 1995; Vuontela et al., 2003).

Research has revealed that parts of the brain do not develop in the same way or at the same rate in females as in males. It appears that the left side of the brain, especially the areas devoted to language, develops first in girls, and the right side of the brain, especially the areas devoted to spatial skills, develops first in boys (Shucard & Shucard, 1990). It is probably the early left-hemisphere development that is responsible for the early advantage that girls have in verbal skills (Njemanze, 2007). So contrary to popular opinion, girls are left-brained, or at least that half of their brain develops first.

Amygdala and Hippocampus

Other parts of the brain show gender differences in development, particularly two small parts of the brain below the cerebrum—the amygdala and the hippocampus. The amygdala is one of several structures deep within the brain associated with emotions, and the hippocampus, usually associated with memory, is located close to the amygdala. A longitudinal study observing developing brains of children ages 4 to 18 found sex-specific developmental differences in the amygdala and the hippocampus. The results indicated that as the children developed, the hippocampus increased more in females and the amygdala increased significantly more in males (Giedd, Castellanos, Rajapakse, Vaituzis, & Raporport, 1997).

What do the amygdala and hippocampus do specifically? Imaging research revealed that when asked to remember something, females tend to use the left side of the memory portion of the brain (the hippocampus) with verbal strategies while males tend to use the right side of that same structure along with visual strategies (Frings et al., 2006). The amygdala also shows different uses between males and females. In emotionally arousing situations, the right portion of the amygdala in males is activated to improve memory for central details, and in females the left portion of the amygdala works to improve memory for peripheral details (Cahill, 2003). This means that in emotional situations, males may tend to pay attention to the basic facts and females may have a more global view of the event.

The amygdala is involved in helping us produce and interpret emotion. Children were shown pictures of people whose faces were exhibiting fear. As females matured, the portion of their brain that processed this information shifted from the amygdala to the prefrontal section of the frontal lobe, whereas most males continued to use the amygdala for this task (Killgore, Oki, & Yurgelun-Todd, 2001). Remember that the prefrontal lobe helps control impulses and make reasoned decisions. The theory is that young females begin to use language to manage their emotions, whereas young males may simply respond to emotions with emotions.

Table 1.1 contains some information about specific lateral gender differences in the amygdala and the hippocampus.

Table 1.1   Gender Differences in the Amygdala and Hippocampus

	Left Side of Brain (develops first in girls)	Right Side of Brain (develops first in boys)
Hippocampus (memory) (develops faster in girls)	Memory of nouns	Memory of pictures and topography
Amygdala (emotions) (develops faster in boys)	Spelling, reading of words, verbal intellect, and vocabulary	Mathematical calculation and performance

SOURCE: Papanicolaou et al., 2002; Yurgelun-Todd, Killgore, & Cintron, 2003.

This means that females begin processing information in the left side of their brain using language as a framework for memory. Males, on the other hand, begin processing information in the right side of their brain using pictures and emotions to remember events.

SUGGESTIONS FOR APPLYING THE THEORY TO YOUR CLASSROOM

✓ When presenting information to girls in the classroom, begin with a comprehensive discussion of the material before you introduce the details.

  o For younger students, give each pair of students the same number of colored blocks to look at. Ask them what they notice about the blocks. When the class decides how to sort the blocks (usually using color as a guide), ask them how many they have of each color. If you have enough blocks, make sure that you have different shapes of the same color, which will give the students another way to sort the blocks. Help your students see that there are many different ways to sort the same collection of blocks. Using the card game SET provides a similar task.

  o For older students, begin a unit on multiplication by having students talk about what they already know about the subject and discussing the general use of multiplication in a wide variety of areas. Try to get your students to see common elements in areas using the same type of mathematical operation. Then give direct instruction in the method. This approach works especially well in science where students will have some knowledge about the subject being discussed.

✓ Begin all math and science classes with written material and carefully describe every step in a problem. Frequently, those of us who find math and science easy are visual learners and we forget that putting an equation on the board without describing it may not have much meaning for a student who learns best from the written or spoken word.

  o Younger students will want to see the step-by-step directions for a science exercise.

  o Older students will need to read the directions for a lab exercise as homework the night before so that they have time to familiarize themselves with the procedure.

✓ If students have weak spatial skills, help them use their verbal skills to compensate. Books such as *The Greedy Triangle* by Marilyn Burns (1994), *Sir Cumference and the Round Table* by Cindy Neuschwander (1997), and *Anno's Mysterious Multiplying Jar* by Masiachiro and Mitsumasa Ann (1983) are all examples of stories that help young students understand the principles of math and figures. There are many similar books, and your librarian or bookseller will be happy to help you find more.

Corpus Callosum

The corpus callosum is the structure that connects the two halves of the cerebrum. The idea has been proposed that if girls use both halves of their brain for language, then the female corpus callosum should be larger to allow the verbal centers on each side of the brain to communicate.

Research is mixed on this topic because there is a tremendous variation in size, shape, and development of this structure. Another factor is that male brains are, on average, bigger than female brains, and it is difficult to say if the differences in size and shape of the corpus callosum are because of sex or individual development (Fine, Semrud-Clikeman, Keith, Stapleton, & Hynd, 2007; Giedd, Blumenthal, Jeffries, Rajapakse, et al., 1999; Morton & Rafto, 2006). An interesting study that looked at the size of the corpus callosum and its relation to reading skills found that as the area of certain sections increased in size, reading ability increased, especially for women (Fine et al.). This last study would seem to confirm the notion that because women use both sides of their brain for language, their corpus callosum will be larger because of the greater number of connections between the two halves. However, this discussion is ongoing because so few studies agree on whether there are gender differences in size, shape, volume, or area of the corpus callosum. Even though there are no definitive answers yet, I include this information primarily because in the future you may hear a discussion of the importance of the corpus callosum to learning.

Sensory Differences

Aside from the gender differences in the way the brain matures and functions, there are also significant gender differences in the way the senses function. All information, regardless of method of presentation or source, enters the brain through one of the senses, so sensory gender differences will create variations in the way children experience what happens in the classroom.

Hearing

From birth, the female ear is more sensitive to sound and can hear quieter sounds and higher-pitched sounds than can the male ear (Cassidy & Ditty, 2001; Corso, 1959). Boys tolerate louder sounds better than girls do (Elliott, 1971; McFadden, 1998), but girls are better than boys are at determining changes in intensity of sound (Velle, 1987). Infant girls are more responsive to auditory stimulation than are their male age-mates (Velle). Girls may find a noisy classroom distracting, but they are better able to discern emotional state from someone's voice.

SUGGESTIONS FOR APPLYING THE THEORY TO YOUR CLASSROOM

✓ Make sure that your voice works for girls.
  o Very young girls may be startled if you use a loud voice to get students' attention. Flash the lights in the room or develop a hand signal to indicate that students should start paying attention to you.

○ In a coed class with older students, girls with very sensitive ears may do better at the back or on the side of the classroom. I have a loud voice, and I recommend to my students with sensitive hearing that the best place for them to sit is in the very front on my left. When I lecture, I turn slightly to my right, so anyone on my left will not get the full force of my voice. On the other hand, if you have a quiet voice, do not assume that all of your students can hear you.

✓ Young girls sometimes find it difficult to speak loudly in class when they answer questions. Have the whole class stand up as tall as they can, which will allow them to fully use their diaphragms, and respond in unison to questions or to recite some material that has been memorized. This will help girls learn how to speak a bit louder and, in a group, they will be more willing to do so.

Vision

While girls have better auditory acuity, boys have better visual acuity, and while boys tolerate sound better, girls tolerate light better (McGuiness, 1976; Velle, 1987). However, even though boys may see better at a distance, particularly when the object is moving, girls can remember more items in a picture. When girls look at the same picture after some of the items have been moved, they will be more accurate in finding the moved items than boys (Kimura, 2000).

Girls also show better perceptual speed than boys do. This is the ability to look at similar items and locate the one item that is different, a skill that is useful in proofreading. This ability to find errors is one of the reasons girls generally are more willing to check their work (Kimura, 2000; Majeres, 1999). While research indicates that adult males have better visual memory than females, as children, girls have better visual memory, probably because of the differences in brain maturation (Vuontela et al., 2003). Additionally, several areas in vision have significant gender differences as well.

Color Vision. Most individuals identified with color blindness (whether the more common red-green variety or the rarer blue-yellow variety) are male. It is rare for a female student to have imperfect color vision, but the condition does appear in women. Color blindness is not the lack of color vision but the inability to differentiate between the paired colors of either red and green or blue and yellow. Individuals with red-green color blindness frequently can't see a difference in color between the top and bottom lights on a traffic signal, as they may see red and green as the same color. You can use the colors in class as color-blind students will see them, just don't use red and green to differentiate similar items, such as providing a red bin for homework and a green bin for permission slips.

Females will name more colors and use more elaborate words to identify colors than males will (Green & Gynther, 1995). Whether or not females actually see more colors than males, or whether it is just that males don't consider slight differences in colors important has not yet been determined. We know that certain cells in the retina, the parvocellular cells, are important for color vision, but there is no research to find if there is a sex difference in the number of these cells (Snowden, 2002).

When drawing pictures, young girls are likely to use more than 10 predominantly warm and bright colors such as red, yellow, pink, and brown, and create pictures with a lot of detail, usually of people placed as if in a posed photograph. Young boys will use fewer than six colors, which may be cooler or darker such as blue, black, and silver, and the pictures may have vehicles or weapons in them designed to be viewed from above or sideways. The impression of girls' pictures is that they are illustrative or decorative, and boys' pictures are realistic or action oriented (Iijima, Arisaka, Minamoto, & Arai, 2001).

SUGGESTIONS FOR APPLYING THE THEORY TO YOUR CLASSROOM

✓ Girls respond well to the use of color. We will discuss specific uses of color in math and science later, but you will note that girls often like to use colored highlighters and color code their materials.

   o Younger students will quickly learn a color-coding system in a classroom. If you use colored paper to post information, children can learn that yellow sheets contain information for their parents, pink sheets contain information for math class, and the like.

   o Not all girls are neat, and one way to help keep materials organized is to color code everything. My math notebooks were always white and my science ones green. That helped me find them in my bookbag or on my desk. I used colored plastic envelopes to store my papers in, and the color of the envelope matched the color for that class. Using the envelopes does not make me any neater, but it does help keep the material for one class together in my bookbag so that I have fewer places to look for papers.

✓ Using the same color to alert students to information will help girls. Teachers have conventionally used red pens to correct papers, and students generally recognize that red marks on a paper indicate mistakes. You don't have to use red, but changing what color you use to correct papers with may create problems for girls. Not all marks made by teachers on papers are to indicate errors, and if you can manage it, try using other colors when you make suggestions or offer praise. "Good work!" will stand out if you write it in green if the corrections are usually marked in red, remembering that color-blind children may see the corrections and the praise as the same color.

Gazing. Not only do boys and girls see differently for acuity and color, but also they choose to look at different things. One-day-old infants were given a choice to look at either a face or a mosaic of a face, and observers agreed that girls looked at the face and boys looked at the mosaic of a face

(Connellan et al., 2000). When one-year-old infants were exposed to videos of moving objects, girls chose to look at faces and boys chose to look at cars (Lutchmaya & Baron-Cohen, 2002). Boys' preference for looking at moving objects at a distance may be responsible for some of the difficulties they have when learning to read and girls, whose eyes see stationary objects close by, may have an advantage when viewing academic work.

When looking at pictures of faces, girls were better than boys at determining what emotion the individual was feeling. Preschool girls were better able than boys were to select a photograph of a child whose face best portrayed the emotion that was described in a story that had been read to the children (Boyatzis, Chazan, & Ting, 1993). In fact, research indicates that all through adolescence, girls are better at nonverbal processing and at determining emotional states of others from facial expressions and body language (McClure, 2000).

SUGGESTIONS FOR APPLYING THE THEORY TO YOUR CLASSROOM

✓ Subtle facial expressions are usually picked up by girls. Most girls are able to read facial expressions and body language well, and they use that information to help them understand what you are trying to tell them. However, do not count on that as a means to convey information.

○ With younger students, simply ask children what they think you meant to convey. You may be surprised that not every student gets the same message.

○ With older students, if you are teaching health or life science, you can give a lesson on body language and on facial cues. Your students may also be interested to learn about the facial feedback hypothesis—if you smile, you tend to think more positively, and if you frown, you may think more negatively.

✓ When working with girls, place them so that they can see your face. Likewise, do not face the blackboard when you lecture, as girls cannot see your face that way.

○ For younger students, classrooms are frequently arranged in groups with the students facing one other. This means that some students may have their backs to you. Either go to each group to speak to them or have the students turn their chairs around when you are giving directions to the whole class.

○ With older students, I recommend that you use an overhead projector with acetate sheets or use a digital projector to display what you are writing on a tablet-type computer. You can then face your students as you write while the machine projects your notes on a screen.

Spatial Relationships

This topic includes several different skills, some of which may be more problematic for girls and others that show no gender advantage. The reason this information is included is that skills in spatial relations are frequently given as reasons that students do well in STEM courses (Halpern et al., 2007).

- Mental rotation is a skill at which men traditionally excel and involves being able to determine which of several three-dimensional figures are the same as a target figure. What makes the task difficult is that none of the sample figures are in the same orientation as the target (Linn & Petersen, 1985).

Figure 1.1   Example of a Mental Rotation Task

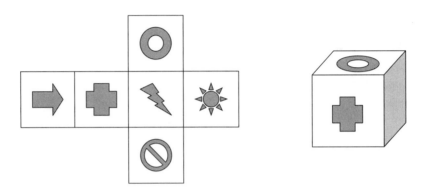

Which image, seen on the flattened cube on the left, would appear in the blank side of the cube on the right? Which image would be on the bottom of the cube?

- Spatial perception is a skill at which men are somewhat better than women. This skill involves being able to determine the relationship of a distant object to one's own body when there is distracting information. An example of this skill is the ability to determine whether a distant line is horizontal if there is a tilted structure on it, such as in Figure 1.2, Ponzo Illusion (Miller, 2001).

Figure 1.2   Ponzo Illusion

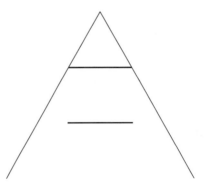

Do the horizontal lines appear to be different in length? Measure the lines to see if you are right.

- Spatial visualization appears to have no gender difference. This skill involves being able to find a simple figure in a complicated one (Linn & Petersen, 1985; Miller, 2001).

Figure 1.3   Example of a Mental Rotation Task

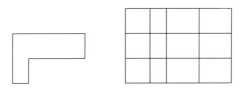

Can you find the simple figure on the left in the more complex figure on the right?

This figure is similar to those on the Embedded Figures Test. Some research indicates that there is no gender difference on this test (Spreen & Strauss, 1998), and other sources report that males are better at finding the hidden figures than females (Jonassen & Grabowski, 1993). While administering this test, I have noticed that men may do a bit better than women, but many women are convinced they can't do it and will say so before beginning the test.

The major issue here is whether or not gender differences in spatial skills affect performance on math and science. Earlier research did not find that spatial skills conveyed an advantage in mathematics but indicated that verbal skills were more highly correlated with math achievement (Friedman, 1995). However, it should be noted that all subjects in the Friedman study were gifted or college-bound students who could be expected to have strong verbal skills. Other studies discovered that performance on a test of mental rotation predicted performance on the SAT-Math (Casey, Nuttall, Pezaris, & Benbow, 1995). More recently, research has uncovered evidence indicating that middle-school girls with poorer spatial-mechanical skills were less likely to do well at the type of math that boys traditionally do extremely well (Casey, Nuttall, & Pezaris, 2001). So do spatial skills make a difference in girls' math performance? Research indicates there may be some influence, teachers I know believe it has a small effect, but my female students are convinced it has a huge influence if they have problems doing well in math, particularly with geometry.

SUGGESTIONS FOR APPLYING THE THEORY TO YOUR CLASSROOM

✓ One way to help girls who are having problems with spatial rotation is to have models of the figures you are discussing.

o For younger students, Cuisenaire rods and other similar block systems are wonderful aids to help explain the principles of algebra and geometry.

(Continued)

(Continued)

    o Most math departments have models for geometric figures and science departments offer models of parts of the body or biological specimens.

✓ Suggest that your students build models for each class.

    o Young children can use bendable straws and tape to construct simple geometric figures both two-dimensional and three-dimensional.

    o Older children can use materials from a craft store to construct models of cells and their organelles. Pipe cleaners, Styrofoam balls or blocks, felt squares, and the like can be used to manufacture the parts of cells or atoms.

    o Another way to build models is to have students become the parts of the model. In the cell model, a different organelle would be assigned to each student who would then become the expert on the function of that organelle. The students would then interact with one another to mimic the actions of the cell.

✓ Any exercise that uses maps will help develop spatial skills. Children can make maps of the classroom, the school, their house, the route from where they live to school, the area where the children live, and many other places as well. Understanding how to develop a drawing that is in the same proportions as the original will help develop spatial skills.

PART 2: THE MIND

It can be a straightforward task to substantiate gender differences in sensory function because there are tests for auditory levels, color vision, spatial skills, and the like. The information about differences in brain maturation comes from magnetic-resonance-imaging (MRI) techniques, which provide tangible results. Evidence about how cognitive skills are influenced by the senses is obtained from eye tests, hearing tests, and other similar tests. However, other differences in cognitive function are more difficult to corroborate because the skills are less evident and the information from visualizing techniques is less specific. For example, there is no single empirical test for verbal skill but rather many tests for various aspects of verbal ability, and most of these tests depend on information gained in school. Vocabulary knowledge, spelling ability, understanding analogies, verbal fluency, and reading facility are just a few of the components of verbal skill. Even though there are gender differences in brain maturation in areas that seem to be involved with verbal skills, many other parts of the brain are also involved when an individual is being tested for verbal ability.

It should be noted that there are greater cognitive differences within sexes than there are between sexes (Halpern, 2000), meaning that males and females differ from their own sex more than they differ from the opposite sex. Consequently, there must be factors other than biology involved in creating these differences. Social pressures, cultural beliefs, parental concerns, and educational expectations are just some of the factors that will affect the development of cognitive gender differences. For example, before 20 months of age, young girls acquire words at a faster rate than young boys (Huttenlocher, Haight, Bryk, Seltzer, & Lyons, 1991). We have already seen that the language centers on the left side of the brain develop early in girls (Shucard & Shucard, 1990), which may account for girls' early verbal skills. Perhaps the reason girls use language so well as they get older is simply that they have more practice. What starts as a sex difference (age at language acquisition) becomes a salient gender trait (girls talk a great deal) that may appear to have been learned through observing adult models, but which begins as the result of interaction between biological traits and environment (Halpern et al., 2007).

The source of gender differences should not matter to teachers whose only concern will be providing educational opportunities to all students in ways that each student learns best. What teachers need is information about how to recognize differences and how to differentiate approaches to learning based on those differences.

Verbal Skills

We have already seen that the topic of verbal skills is a complicated one, and it may be a bit easier to look at this group of skills by breaking it into three subgroups: (1) input of information such as reading and listening, (2) output of information such as writing and speaking, and (3) utilization of information involving knowledge recall and problem solving. The evidence is strong that girls are better than boys in the first two groups of skills. One consideration for why girls suppose that they are going to have trouble with math is that math appears to require skills in the third group where girls believe they are less competent, such as logic and problem solving.

Input of Information

One way for information to enter the brain is by listening, and we have already noted that females are more sensitive to auditory stimuli and are better able to determine differences in volume than males (Velle, 1987). The research on gender differences in auditory memory indicates that females are slightly better than males at retaining information when the stimulus is heard (Geffen, Moar, Hanlon, Clark, & Geffen, 1990; Trahan & Quintana, 1990). This may be the reason why lectures work well as a method to transmit information for most women. If girls have more sensitive hearing, then it follows that receiving information by listening can be an effective learning technique for them. There is some evidence that girls' auditory as well as their visual working memory develops before that of boys (Vuontela et al., 2003).

Verbal memory, on the other hand, is quite clearly better for girls than for boys. Most females are better at reading comprehension and have better memory for words than males (Halpern, 2000; Kimura, 2000). It is interesting that when subjects were asked to match words based on their physical characteristics such as length and shape there were no gender differences in speed. On the other hand, when the task involved the sound of words, women were faster than men. These tasks involve reading words out loud, and females have an advantage when the spelling of words is similar, such as sweat and treat, or the words were pseudohomophones, such as brane or selery (Majeres, 1999). The explanation for this difference is that girls have better phonological processing than boys, which means that girls can decipher the sound of words better.

SUGGESTIONS FOR APPLYING THE THEORY TO YOUR CLASSROOM

✓ Lecture is a teaching style that generally works with girls because they learn well from the spoken word.

  o For young children, make sure that you accompany what you say by showing your students what you are talking about. They need to start to learn to use the written word as well as the spoken word as sources of information.

  o Dictation is an excellent way to find out if your students are hearing what you say. Some students are better at remembering spoken words than others, and it will help all students to practice transcribing oral directions.

✓ Do not assume that all girls learn well from lecture, so make sure that you also provide information in written form as well. When a student cannot follow your spoken directions, it may be that the student is not paying attention, but it may also be that the student does not easily process spoken words.

✓ Some girls are so good at listening that they may not write anything down. Help these students learn to take some notes to help jog their memories. Suggest that, as they read the textbook, they note information from class discussion that elaborates or supports what is in the book. If students are not allowed to write in books, they may write these notes on sticky notes and place the notes over the paragraph.

Output of Information

Girls have an advantage in understanding and remembering words, and also, they are generally better than boys at producing words. Verbal fluency is measured by counting the total number of words beginning with a certain letter that can be produced in one minute. Females, particularly school-age girls, can produce more words under these conditions than their male age-mates (Kramer, Delis, Kaplan, O'Donnell, & Prifitera, 1997; Spreen & Strauss, 1998). That simply means that girls can get words out faster when speaking, but there is no difference between females and males in verbal intelligence, understanding the meaning of words (Halpern, 2000).

In writing, girls appear to have better skills than boys. A study pointed out that one reason girls do well on the free-response portion of the U. S. History Advanced Placement exams is that their English composition skills are superior (Breland, Danos, Kahn, Kubota, & Bonner, 1994). Even though females may write more fluidly and with better organization, males are still more likely to earn a living as writers (Halpern, 2000). For example, in 2005, only 18.8% of film writers and 27.2% of television writers were women (Hunt, 2007). It would be pure speculation to give a reason why women are not represented fairly in the writing professions as a whole because girls generally have the edge in writing skills.

SUGGESTIONS FOR APPLYING THE THEORY TO YOUR CLASSROOM

✓ Give girls the opportunity to write as a way to help them learn the material in the class.

- o If a young girl has trouble solving a particular variety of math problems, have her use words to write down the steps in the process. That may help her see the order of the steps in the problem.
- o One reason for lab reports in science is to help the verbal student process the events that transpired in the laboratory exercise and write down those events in a logical, systematic fashion. The student who has strong verbal skills will benefit from using that strength to organize information that was not collected from a verbal source. If a female student has trouble organizing her thoughts, require that she outline the lab report based on the order of events.

✓ Journaling is traditionally required to help students organize their thoughts.

- o For long-term projects, keeping a journal will help all students remember what happened during the progress of the project as well as provide a place to jot down facts for future use. Keeping lab journals is an excellent way for students to process what has happened during a long-term exercise.
- o Math journals can help students work through math problems by giving them a place to write out their difficulties. A sample entry might look like this: "I'm having trouble remembering how to enter a polynomial into my calculator. All of the various parentheses simply make the problem more complicated, but if I don't get them right, the answer is usually wrong. It helps if I write the problem with the parentheses before entering it in the calculator."

✓ In science, have students develop questions from classwork or labwork. Learning to rephrase information so that it asks a question rather than answers one helps students use verbal skills to remember information gained from an activity.

Knowledge Recall and Problem Solving

The stereotype for knowledge recall is that boys remember more facts, and that is particularly true if it is in an area that interests them (Ackerman, Bowen, Beier, & Kanfer, 2001; Henrie, Aron, Nelson, & Poole, 1997; Lynn & Irwing, 2002). However, women have better verbal memory, particularly when the task is simple memorization (Martins et al., 2005) or if the task concerns memory for episodes (Halpern, 2000; Lewin, Wolgers, & Herlitz, 2001). That means that women can learn more information intentionally through rote memorization or when the information is made relevant to some event.

SUGGESTIONS FOR APPLYING THE THEORY TO YOUR CLASSROOM

✓ Point out to your students that while memorizing formulas and other facts may seem to provide a foolproof method for being correct, if they can't remember or make mistakes in recall, they will not get the right answer. Help your students figure out what is the least amount of material needed to derive all the information needed. Learning to solve problems is much better than memorizing all the answers.

✓ Learning information by heart is a method many girls depend on, especially in science and math. Although this seems admirable, if the problem is not exactly like the one the student memorized, she may have trouble recognizing it.

  o I have known students to memorize the formulas for determining speed, distance, and rate when these are just different versions of the same formula. Help your students to learn to figure out how to use one formula to find related others rather than letting them memorize each separate formula. The ability to use one formula to find another will be valuable in the years to come.

  o Many girls who have trouble with geometry have passed the course simply by memorizing the process for every type of proof. Help your students see the logical progression of the proof rather than depending on memory.

    o Help them see the pattern in a proof—it always starts with the given information.

    o Teach them how to solve problems backward by starting from the statement that you are trying to prove and moving toward the statement at the beginning.

    o Some of my students had problems with the shorthand developed to save space in proofs, such as SAS for *side, angle, side,* and preferred to write out the whole name of the theorem because seeing the words helped them frame the proof.

If the information requires visuospatial processing, such as graphs, charts, formulas, or geometric figures, it has been thought that men are better able to remember that information simply through visualization of the information (Lewin et al., 2001). One study suggested that more women were object visualizers, remembering static pictures, and more men were spatial visualizers, remembering information by manipulating or transforming the images (Harshman & Paivio, 1987). A later study did support the two types of visualizers but did not find the same gender differentiation (Kozhevnikov, Kosslyn, & Shephard, 2005). This study determined that object visualizers solve problems holistically by looking at the entire problem, whereas spatial visualizers solve problems by analyzing the various elements in the problem. The point was made that both types of visualizers perform equally well on the quantitative section of the SAT and can solve science problems equally well, albeit from a different perspective. According to the latest information in this area, there may not be any gender differences in the style of visualization.

SUGGESTIONS FOR APPLYING THE THEORY TO YOUR CLASSROOM

✓ In math and science classes, present information for both types of visualizers by helping them find patterns in the problems. Object visualizers will benefit when the lesson gives set solutions to a problem type. Spatial visualizers will benefit when the lesson encourages the students to break the problem into different steps that can then be approached from different perspectives.

   o It is important to start this process very early. Have very young students use geoboards to help them visualize patterns and shapes.

   o Use tessellations to show that patterns can emerge by coloring the designs in repetitive ways.

   o Older students can use logic puzzles, chess, and other games to help them see how to use the parts of a problem to come to a solution.

✓ Pair students up and have one student describe something to the other who then has to draw it. Both students learn about visualization because the describer has to translate an object into words that will make sense to the student who is drawing. The student who draws has to translate words into pictures on the page.

✓ Prepare girls for standardized tests by giving them sample items requiring visualization. Analyze the different types of items and, as a class, develop different approaches for each type of question.

   o All students can learn to categorize problems by finding key words in the problem, which gives some direction to the method that will work best to solve the problem. For example, if the problem asks for the total number of items, addition is required to arrive at the answer.

The other issues in this area are problem-solving approaches and logic skills. The diversity between girls and boys in this area makes a huge difference in the way that they answer problems, but whether these differences are innate or learned is not clear. This is an area where teachers would like to know if these differences are acquired or built into the way brains function. If students learn problem-solving strategies, they can be taught to use specific approaches. If the approaches that students use are part of the way their brains operate, then the teacher must help students find different methods using their own inborn strategies as a framework.

The stereotype is that girls and boys do not always use the same strategies in mathematical problem solving. A study of first graders found that girls were very concerned about getting the right answer, and to do so they would use methods such as counting on their fingers to insure that they were correct. Boys in this study were more likely simply to retrieve information even though they did not always arrive at the correct answer. What is interesting is that the number of correct responses was about the same for both girls and boys (Carr & Jessup, 1997). Another study with similar results revealed that girls in Grades 1 through 3 were more likely to solve problems using concrete strategies such as using tallies, and boys in the same classes were more likely to solve problems using more abstract solution approaches involving concepts (Fennema, Carpenter, Jacobs, Franke, & Levi, 1998).

By sixth grade, girls were less sure of their ability to solve problems and were more likely than boys to ascribe their mistakes to a lack of proficiency in math. However, the girls in this study, even though they were not convinced of their math ability, were more likely than the boys to continue to work on a problem, whereas the boys were more likely to give up (Vermeer, Boekaerts, & Seegers, 2000).

The gender differences in problem-solving strategies continue through high school, and a study of students who performed well on standardized tests revealed some of those differences when those students were asked to solve items from the SAT-M. The items were classified as conventional when the method of solving the problem was clear using an algorithm or as unconventional when the method of solving the problem might require estimation, insight, or some creative use of more conventional methods but was not an approach that had been taught in class. On these problems, female students were more likely to use conventional strategies, and male students were more likely to use unconventional strategies (Gallagher & De Lisi, 1994). This confirmed an earlier study that proposed that female students were more likely to use strategies they had been taught in class (Kimball, 1989).

SUGGESTIONS FOR APPLYING THE THEORY TO YOUR CLASSROOM

✓ It is tempting to teach students one way to solve problems. This takes less time and most students will do well. The problem arises when the problem on the standardized test does not look exactly like the ones covered in class. When that happens, girls may have trouble.

o Give groups of students different problems to solve. Then have each group come to the front of the room and show their classmates how to solve the problem. That will allow you to cover more material, and when students come up with novel methods, you will have the chance to help the class learn new approaches.

○ If a student asks how to solve a problem, don't tell her immediately. Ask her what she thinks is the way to solve it. Frequently, girls are just looking for affirmation that they are on the correct path and, if you tell them how to do it, they may not learn to develop their own methods.

✓ Before you include questions on your own tests that can be solved in unconventional ways, give the class similar items for homework or as a class exercise. Let students work together to develop novel solutions. Yes, you need to prepare your students for the state-standard exams, but knowing how to use information in an innovative way will solidify understanding much more than just learning to identify what problems require certain solution approaches. If items on the standard exams do not look exactly like the ones studied in class, knowing a variety of solution paths will increase your students' chances of solving the problems.

The conclusion to be drawn from these studies is that when doing math problems, female students are more likely to work hard, to be very concerned that they use the right procedure, to use strategies that they have been taught in class, and to be less sure of their ability to be successful in math. This certainly describes many of my female students who worked hard, but if they could not match a problem with a solution they were familiar with, they would state that they did not know how to solve the problem. When I prodded them to come up with new approaches, the girls would point out that they had learned a certain method and that was how they were going to solve the problem. The older the student, the more resistant she was to coming up with a different way of solving the problem. The chapter on math will give many ideas and strategies to help girls overcome this mindset.

Analytic Styles

Another skill related to problem solving is the approach that is used to analyze information. One theory is that the male brain is wired to predict behavior by analyzing systems and understanding the principles that control them. In this model, the female brain is wired to predict behavior by empathizing with others and understanding them (Baron-Cohen, 2003). The empathizer must be connected in some way to others to work with them, whereas the systemizer needs to see others in a detached way to understand them. This theory is one explanation of why women are likely to follow the directions of superiors and men will try to figure out what superiors want from them before they act.

This model might explain why males perform better on standardized tests and females do better on teacher-made tests, especially in high school math (Kimball, 1989). Girls are more likely to pay close attention to what the teacher finds important and prepare for that material on the test.

Boys, on the other hand, are frequently astounded at what they find on a teacher-made test and will remark that the teacher never told them what material they would be responsible for knowing. On standardized tests, boys can use their systemizing skills to analyze a problem and figure out how to solve it while the girls spend time trying to relate the problem to ones they have seen in class. My female students would return after taking the SAT-M and remark that they probably did badly because they didn't recognize any questions on the test from work we had done in class, and then when they found out their score, they were astounded at how well they had done.

SUGGESTIONS FOR APPLYING THE THEORY TO YOUR CLASSROOM

✓ Make sure that you prepare your students for standardized tests by helping them learn general problem-solving techniques for all sorts of problems. The important part of these strategies is to get students to work independently and to realize that there is a myriad of possible solutions.

   o This works well when the approach starts when students are very young. Give groups of students several objects, such as a soccer ball, a piece of paper, a length of rope, and a chair, and challenge them to get each member of the group from one side of a room to another without touching the floor.

   o Older students can be given a theoretical problem to solve, such as figuring out how a family of four can live on a particular income.

✓ Remember that not all students approach problem solving in the same way. Girls can get confused if you present alternative approaches, thinking that they have to learn all of the ways that you demonstrate. Make it clear to your students that if an alternative problem-solving method is confusing they don't need to try to learn that method as long as they are successful with another strategy.

✓ Approach all problems in the classroom as avenues to teach or model problem solving. Be purposeful about this by remarking that the problem exists and that the class can solve the problem on their own. Problems can range from how to decide who will be the "person of the day" in an elementary class to how to study for an exam with an older class.

While girls may not do as well as boys on the SAT-M, on other standardized tests, such as the National Assessment of Educational Progress (NAEP), the difference between girls and boys is either not significant or, in some cases, girls are doing better. In 2005, 12th-grade boys only scored two points higher than 12th-grade girls on math. However, in the same year, girls' scores in reading averaged 13 points higher than those of boys.

These results indicate that it is not necessarily the standardized nature of a test that is the reason girls don't do as well as boys in math (National Center for Educational Statistics [NCES], 2007b).

Recent information has linked the gender gap in math to the gender gap index of the World Economic Forum. In gender-equal countries, girls scored as well as or better than boys in math (Guiso, Monte, Sapienza, & Zingales, 2008). Certainly, in math some of the differences between girls and boys are because of social inequities, and the more girls obtain social parity, the better their math scores become.

BRAIN AND COGNITIVE DIFFERENCES

Those in the scientific fields are beginning to understand that the brains of females and males do not function identically and that those differences result in gender-specific ways of thinking (Halpern et al., 2007). At the same time, we are very aware of the influence that society has on what we believe we can do, which can give us confidence to persevere or convince us we should not even try. Teachers who understand the basics of cognitive gender differences will be better able to frame lessons for all of their students.

ANSWERS TO QUIZ

1. A—Girls can hear whispers very well (Cassidy & Ditty, 2001; Corso, 1959; McFadden, 1998).

2. B—Boys are more comfortable when the room is colder, even though it may be hard to get adolescent girls to put on a sweater when they get cold (Beshir & Ramsey, 1981).

3. C—Boys and girls have equal activity levels. This is true as long as you are talking about children younger than 24 months. After that, boys seem to be more active, but even then, the level of activity varies a great deal and depends on the situation and on the expectation of activity levels (Maccoby, 1998).

4. B—Boys see moving objects better, particularly if the moving object is a car (Lutchmaya & Baron-Cohen, 2002)!

5. A—Girls have more connections between neurons in the brain. The suggestion is made that the female brain tends to consider facts in context rather than as individual bits of information (de Courten-Myers, 1999).

6. A—Girls' left side of their brain matures sooner than boys'. It is the left side of the brain where verbal processing begins and the right side of the brain that begins the development of spatial skills (Shucard & Shucard, 1990).

(Continued)

(Continued)

7. B—Boys can throw objects at a target better than girls can at an earlier age. For example, few boys can be persuaded to drop trash in the receptacle; they have to toss it in as if they are shooting a basketball (Halpern, 2000).

8. B—Boys have a higher tolerance for pain than girls do. Boys may whine and complain more, but girls report feeling higher levels of pain to the same stimuli (Jackson, Iezzi, Gunderson, Nagasaka, & Fritch, 2002).

9. B—Boys use primarily visual strategies to remember while females use both verbal and visual systems, though the ability to remember was similar for both (Frings et al., 2006).

10. A—Girls are more likely to use concrete strategies and boys use more abstract methods to solve arithmetic problems in first grade, but they achieved the same grades.

2

Differences in Learning Approaches

SOURCE: Photographer: Duane Berger. Used with permission.

One side of a discussion about cognitive gender differences assumes that those differences will have an effect on how the individual processes information. If people have strong verbal skills, they are likely to read and listen well. People who have good spatial skills may find it easier to learn if the information is presented in a chart or graph. Most individuals can learn in a variety of ways, but a good number of us have preferred methods. The way the individual prefers to process information will determine what avenue will result in the most efficient learning.

Are there gender-specific approaches to learning? See how well you do in answering the following questions about how males and females learn differently.

QUIZ

Respond to the following statements by indicating whether the statement best describes (a) girls, (b) boys, or (c) both girls and boys.

1. Are more likely to be identified as generally learning disabled

2. Are more likely to be identified with a math disability

3. Are effectively able to define a problem and select the appropriate strategy

4. Spend more time after school on homework or studying

5. Learn best with peers because of their orientation to others

6. Have peer groups that are less likely to be study oriented

7. Have better proofreading skills

8. Are more willing to check for errors and correct mistakes

9. Are less likely to use a variety of strategies to solve problems

10. Have a more realistic view of academic success and failure

Answers are on page 49.

Some teachers may not be completely persuaded that variations in the ways that girls and boys learn are based on cognitive gender differences. Their doubts may be based on the belief that girls and boys learn the way that they do because they were taught to study in a certain way. Certainly, that is part of the picture, but having taught in both girls' and boys' schools, I am convinced that many of the ways that children choose to learn are the result of their individual experiences in the classroom molded by their underlying cognitive gender differences. That means teachers need to be responsive to gender differences when planning academic activities, keeping in mind that what works for the teacher may not work for the student.

As a female with a brain that functions in many respects more like a male brain, I have learned not to assume that the sex of the child is necessarily indicative of how the child approaches learning. My learning disabilities are more similar to the boys I have taught than to the girls; I am terrible at spelling and auditory processing, which means that can I relate to many of the problems that my male students have in school. However, I am female, and my verbal abilities are more similar to those of my female students, so I understand some about how they approach academic work. Few of us are entirely one way or the other, and you will find some students whose way of working resembles the descriptions that follow and others who don't fit at all. Overall, you will find that more of your female students will match than not.

LEARNING MODALITIES

In this context, modality is a term that indicates the sensory sources of information, so learning modalities refer to learning when the source is ears (auditory), eyes (visual-verbal and visual-iconic), and hands (kinesthetic).

- Auditory learning occurs when the information is *heard.* Sources of auditory information are lectures, movies, seminars, small-group work, debates, or anytime that the individual is listening to information—actually, this involves much of what goes on in a classroom.
- Visual-verbal learning occurs when the information is *read.* Sources of visual-verbal information are books; handouts; information written on a blackboard, whiteboard, or SMART Board; PowerPoint presentations; or anytime that the individual is reading words.
- Kinesthetic learning occurs when the information is *manipulated.* Sources of kinesthetic information are lab exercises, taking notes, acting, singing, working problems, building models, conducting research, or anytime the individual is doing something with the material.
- Visual-iconic learning occurs when the information is *seen* but words are not central to the presentation of the information. Sources of visual-iconic information are charts, tables, graphs, pictures, demonstrations, movies, or anytime that the individual sees information presented in a pictorial or graphic fashion.

Auditory Learning

There is not a lot of research in this area, but it would seem that if a student easily accesses information through one of the sensory systems, that will be a good learning approach for that student. We know that girls' hearing is more acute than boys, so auditory information should be easier for girls to remember, and we have already seen that girls have better auditory memory than boys (Geffen, Moar, Hanlon, Clark, & Geffen, 1990; Vuontela et al., 2003).

There is a confounding factor in the statement, "Girls have better auditory memory," because what may actually be assessed is verbal memory. If the material to be remembered is presented in words, there is always the possibility that it is not the auditory but the verbal nature of the information that is the source of the female advantage in remembering what is heard. Because most information heard in a classroom involves words, teachers may believe that most female students will have better auditory memory than male students. However, as a female with lousy auditory memory, please know that if a student can't tell you what you just said, it may not be because the student wasn't paying attention but because the student doesn't remember auditory information, even though the information involves words. Believe me, there is a difference, and if I'm going to remember what I hear, I have to write it down. What this means for teachers is that verbal presentation of information is a good method to teach girls, but not all girls.

SUGGESTIONS FOR APPLYING THE THEORY TO YOUR CLASSROOM

✓ Make sure that you provide written directions or explanations no matter how clear you think you are in describing what the students are expected to do. Students who have poor auditory-processing skills will need to have another source to make sure that they get the information.

   o For young students, you will need to post directions or write them on the board.
   o For older students, you may use a Web site as a source of information. You can post homework assignments, extra material, links to other Web sites, and a lot of other information that can be read.

✓ Teach all students to take competent notes. Even if a female student is a good auditory learner, she will need to know how to convert information from an auditory source to a written record.

   o For young students, start by giving directions and asking the students to write down a summary of the directions. This will help you discover if any children have subtle hearing problems or auditory processing issues, but also, it gives children practice in getting the gist of what the teacher says, not necessarily the exact words.
   o Older girls will typically prefer to take notes in a linear fashion; however, some may be more visual and will relate better to webbing or charting. If you are not familiar with these techniques, ask the learning specialist in your school for assistance.
   o Although reading to students may not seem to be part of a math and science curriculum, giving students practice in listening will help develop auditory skills. In science, you might read about an animal and then have students draw a picture of it. By asking students to use nonverbal skills, you help students develop all of the means of acquiring information.

Verbal Learning

We discussed previously that the source of the female verbal advantage may be the result of their earlier left-sided brain development. Girls read earlier than boys and with greater confidence, although, certainly, you are going to find girls who have trouble reading in middle school and boys who are facile readers before they get to kindergarten. Frequently, what you will find is that girls will want to read about any topic you introduce in class in preference to any other method of acquiring information (Buck & Ehlers, 2002), so make sure that students have access to the material in written form.

SUGGESTIONS FOR APPLYING THE THEORY TO YOUR CLASSROOM

✓ Introduce material through verbal means: provide written information, tell a story, describe the material, and so forth.

✓ Act as a scribe for very young students to enable them to put into words an event or experience in class. Part of that exercise is developing their vocabulary, which helps them describe visual events.

✓ If the information is graphically presented or demonstrated to the class, make sure that you give a running commentary so that the girls have words to associate with the picture or visually presented material.

✓ If you teach young children, do not assume that all girls are facile readers. The girl who is a poor reader will be uncomfortable if she is identified by the class as having problems with reading. Make sure that she gets help in an unobtrusive way. If you have students read out loud in class, let this student prepare a passage in advance. No one has to know that the student was already familiar with the material.

Kinesthetic Learning

Kinesthetic learning tends to be more difficult for girls, as many are not inclined to manipulate materials. I found it difficult to get my female students to examine the parts of plants and reluctant to dissect specimens in a biology lab exercise. They would rather look at pictures in a book or look at someone else manipulating the material. Research supports that, in a science laboratory, girls were less likely to use tools in a novel way and more likely to follow carefully the directions of the teacher (Jones et al., 2000). However, once my students got used to laboratory exercises, they enjoyed them and learned a great deal through that method. I did not push them, but I did not do the dissections for them.

One reason girls may be less inclined to manipulate materials in class may be because of their lower level of impulsivity when compared to boys of the same age. There is lots of evidence that boys are more impulsive and are more likely to get physically involved in a class activity (Baron-Cohen, 2003; Honigsfeld & Dunn, 2003). It may be that in a coed classroom, girls are less inclined to become actively involved because the boys are so involved. In single-sex math classes, girls reported that they were better able to learn math because their greater involvement helped them become more comfortable with the material. The boys in the same study did not find that the single-sex format made a difference in their math performance (Seitsinger, Barboza, & Hird, 1998).

This is somewhat surprising given the fact that girls have better fine-motor skills earlier than boys (Kimura, 2000), so it might seem that girls would be more willing to touch and handle materials in the classroom. One reason for girls' preference for not interacting physically with class materials comes from the belief that girls are more willing to please the teacher (Maccoby, 1998; Pomerantz, Altermatt, & Saxon, 2002), and if the teacher says, "Don't touch," girls are more likely to obey. Another reason is that boys are more impulsive (James, 2007) and may simply take over the lab exercise.

SUGGESTIONS FOR APPLYING THE THEORY TO YOUR CLASSROOM

✓ Encourage girls to become physically involved with the manipulatives of a class exercise. In a coed class, you can divide students into groups by gender, but if you would prefer not to, provide some guidelines for a minimum amount of interaction with the material.

  o Younger students may be more willing to become physically involved in a class exercise. Keep watch to make sure that the girls are an active part of the assignment. If girls consistently let boys take over, assign specific tasks for each child in the group.

  o For older students, be careful that a girl does not always volunteer to be the scribe as her major contribution to the group effort. The rest of the students may be perfectly happy to let her do so. All students, even those with bad handwriting, need to learn to write down results or information from research.

✓ Make sure that if you use manipulatives in a math class that all students are taking part, as some girls may be tempted simply to observe others. Keep a chart of student interactions, and make sure that at least once each week each female student demonstrates to you that she is able to use the manipulative being studied.

✓ For upper-level science courses, have a lab-practical exam as part of the grade for the course. This will show students that it is important for them to get involved in the lab exercises and will allow students who are good at these skills a place to shine.

Visual Learning

Although most girls will remember well what they read, their memory for what they see is not as clear-cut. There is information that indicates that males are better at visual memory and visual learning in general (Martins et al., 2005), although other information implies that visual memory in girls matures before that of boys (Vuontela et al., 2003). The latter study may provide an explanation for the observation that women are clearly faster than men at perceptual speed, which is the ability to compare shapes and patterns such as letters, numbers, or pictures (Kimura, 2000). Here, visual memory is used as the individual scans the designs to remember what the target looks like to find the similar one. This skill is used to find differences between two similar pictures or to proofread. One theory is that women assign names to each of the symbols or designs and, therefore, turn a visual-memory task into a verbal one.

Some tests of visual memory, such as memory for object locations, have shown an advantage for women (Halpern, 2000). However, these results are not clear and other research shows that men may be better in object location than women (Cattaneo, Postma, & Vecchi, 2006; de Goede, Kessels, & Postma, 2006). If the information is presented graphically, it is likely that men will remember more material (Geiger & Litwiller, 2005). Men seem to have better visuospatial memory, a skill useful in computer games, as it involves movement in space and time; in one study, men were better able to determine what shape will result when two separate shapes are combined (Lawton & Hatcher, 2005).

Figure 2.1   Test of Visuospatial Memory

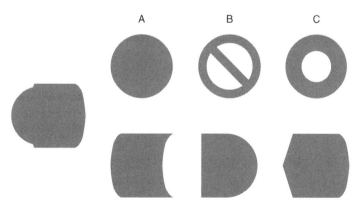

When combined, which set of shapes (A, B, or C) will result in the shape at the left?

Why am I interested in how well girls remember things other than words? In working with my students, I have found that remembering graphic and iconic data can be difficult for some girls—or at least they believe that it is difficult for them to remember such information. Part of the problem that some girls have with beginning algebra in particular is that they find the notation bewildering. First, the mix of numbers and letters to stand for variables is confusing—what does $4x$ stand for? To a verbally oriented student, the most important part of that term may be the letter, which should have some connection to a word, but here it plainly doesn't. Some girls find the repetitive use of x and y for variables confusing, especially if two successive problems use the same notation for unknowns.

SUGGESTIONS FOR APPLYING THE THEORY TO YOUR CLASSROOM

✓ If a girl is having trouble recognizing that the letters stand for variables, use your pencil to make a mark across each similar variable. Marking the variables is something I only do with students who are having trouble, and then only long enough for them to understand that the letters are standing for variables.

✓ Another strategy is to use a highlighter to make a dot over similar variables. Using different colors can be very useful when the problems involve more than one variable. For example,

  ○ $22 - 3x = 8x$ for one variable equations, or
  ○ $3x + 4y = 12 - 2y + 2x$ for two variable equations.

✓ Approach mathematical and scientific symbols as pictures that can show what it is they represent rather than mixed up letters. For example, the formula for sugar is $C_6H_{12}O_6$. Draw the hexagonal shape of the molecule so that the students can see how the letters and numbers fit together.

✓ In math, bring in real apples and oranges (or anything to stand in for different objects) and arrange them as in the equation. In the example earlier, use small blocks to stand in for the numbers. Use a big block for the variable and little blocks for the numbers. Put out the blocks as indicated in the problem—22 little blocks, 3 big blocks, and 8 big blocks. Let the students move the blocks around until they can see what value each big block has to have to make the equation work.

I have also found that some of my female students, particularly those in pre-algebra, find the symbols for operations baffling especially when the material gets beyond basic arithmetic terms. For example, what does -4 mean? Does that mean that you are to subtract four from something else, or does it mean that the value of the term is less than zero? How do you read -4? Is it minus four or negative four? The verbal descriptions are not the same as one indicates an operation and the other indicates a value. To an individual who focuses on words, that creates a problem. To someone who focuses on the numbers, it doesn't matter whether you are subtracting a quantity or whether that quantity has a negative value, as the effect is pretty much the same in a simple add/subtract equation. If a quantity is being multiplied by or divided by -4, then some students may have trouble understanding that the sign of the number indicates a value and not an operation.

One day, a student interrupted the lesson in class when she asked what the difference was between minus and negative. I pointed out that subtracting a positive four or adding a negative four gave the same result. She was still confused, and when I realized that the whole class was having problems with this at some level, I put a number line at the top of the board. I used it to help clarify each instance of this situation as it came up in the material until they all got comfortable with the ambiguous terminology. As you clarify this ambiguity, make sure that your students are comfortable with both meanings of the term as there are places when either one or the other is needed. For one pre-algebra class that was having particular trouble, I required them all to put a number line at the top of every test and use it to determine how to combine numbers until they were all able to do so easily.

Here is the crux of the matter, some terms in math and science are indeed ambiguous, and that creates difficulties for a student who is word oriented. Minus and negative are simply the tip of the iceberg. How about multiply and times? Is there a difference between twice and multiply by two or divide by and divide into? Does the delta symbol indicate change or heat? If a student remembers words best, the student needs to be clear on what the words mean. If girls have trouble with the symbols in math, they will ask questions such as, "What does that letter stand for?" or "Why does this problem use the same letters as an earlier problem? Do they have the same meaning or value?"

The research on memory and object location also gives a clue as to why some girls have trouble with the more graphic nature of math and science. If the reason women remember the location of objects is that they give names to the objects, then remembering the formula for glucose, which is $C_6H_{12}O_6$, may be difficult unless the formula is introduced as "Carbon six, hydrogen twelve, oxygen six." When I taught science in a girls' school, I always said the full name of each element as I wrote the formula on the board. I found it helped some of my students to be reminded of the names of the elements, even though we wrote $C_6H_{12}O_6$. As they became more familiar with the formulas, I just read what I wrote and did not give the full name of each element.

SUGGESTIONS FOR APPLYING THE THEORY TO YOUR CLASSROOM

✓ Do not be tempted to shortcut the names of terms when you write them until you are sure that every student in the class understands what you mean. While helping a girl learn to balance chemical equations, I discovered that she had no idea what the arrow meant (you will remember that it indicates a chemical reaction occurs).

✓ For students who are having trouble remembering the meaning of symbols, have them develop a chart or list of the symbols with their meaning. Do not be tempted to do this for them; it is making the list that helps them remember what the symbols stand for.

✓ Use physical objects, such as blocks, to stand in for variables in equations to help students understand what x stands for in an equation.

GROUP SIZE

When I talk to teachers about girls' group size, I usually get grins and lots of examples of what happens when you put an odd number of girls together to work on a project. Teachers are amazed when I tell them that there is research to back up their observations, and the research is very clear that girls work better in groups composed of even numbers. The reason given is that females focus on individuals in a group, so if they are in a group larger than two, the other people in the group may feel left out, as they are not receiving attention (Benenson & Heath, 2006). This is probably because of the focus on faces shown by infant girls, which was mentioned earlier.

If you have three girls working in a group, the likelihood is that two will focus on each other and the third student will not be included. Groups of four allow for pairs of girls to work together. I have seen three girls working together quite effectively, but it is the exception rather than the rule. If three girls ask to work together, give them the benefit of the doubt until you can observe whether all three are equal partners in the enterprise. I've also seen two girls who weren't very motivated or capable pick a lonely third girl who can do the work. The attention of the two is flattering to the one until she realizes that she is carrying the entire load.

SUGGESTIONS FOR APPLYING THE THEORY TO YOUR CLASSROOM

✓ If you need to have three girls work together, make sure that the tasks are well defined. That way, each student knows what she is to do and it will be obvious to all if one girl is trying to get someone else to do her work.

✓ If your class size requires that you use groups larger than two, make sure that the girls change groups on a regular basis. As new groups are started, girls will learn how to do different jobs. Also, if one group of girls is particularly toxic, moving students regularly will provide relief for the group that does not get along.

✓ It also helps to give two grades for group work, one grade for the project and another grade for individual effort. That will encourage all students to put forth a more equal amount of effort.

FAIRNESS

"It's not fair!" Every teacher has heard this complaint from students. Girls believe that effort is the measure of success, so a problem may occur if a child who spent three hours on an assignment gets a lower grade than a classmate who spent 20 minutes on the same assignment. The earlier all students learn that work is judged not on the amount of time spent preparing it but on the end result, the easier your task will be. This is another reason to grade with rubrics or other methods that clarify the standards for success.

In an attempt to help girls who focus on effort, teachers may give some credit or modify a grade when a student indicates that she spent a good deal of time preparing the assignment. Only do that if the rubric allows effort to improve a grade. Unless students learn this early, they may be surprised, particularly in college, when the teacher is only interested in the final product. I am convinced this is part of the issue that some girls have with math and science—the answer is the answer. The amount of time you spend getting it is not important. I have had girls tell me that they like courses where essay questions are given, as they believe that the teacher will give more points for longer answers—effort pays off.

Another issue with fairness is how rules are used to apply discipline. Girls believe that induction works best in dealing with misbehavior (Barnett, Quackenbush, & Sinisi, 1996). Induction is the method by which the adult or person in authority points out that another person has been hurt by the young offender and asks how the offender would feel if someone did the same thing to him or her. The focus of induction may center on how the misbehavior affects an adult, either parent or teacher—"I'm disappointed in your behavior"—or on how the misbehavior affects the victim—"How do you think that makes Suzie feel?" Girls feel that parent-oriented induction is more fair than victim-oriented induction (Horton, Ray, & Cohen, 2001). So not only do girls find induction a more fair way to discipline, but also they find that it is more fair to point out how the misbehavior affects the parent or other adult rather than the victim. The rules apply, but circumstances may mean that the application of the rules changes depending on the effect of the misbehavior. This is another instance of effort making a difference for girls.

For girls, fairness is a matter of listening to all sides and making the most equitable decision for all.

SUGGESTIONS FOR APPLYING THE THEORY TO YOUR CLASSROOM

✓ Rubrics for grading are essential in math and science, and they will make it much easier to help students see what they need to do and how their efforts are going to be graded. Give older students the rubrics for long-term assignments at the beginning so that they can see where to focus their efforts.

✓ Do not let students present work, especially lab reports, in elaborate report covers or in binders that are there for more than just keeping the work together. I have had subpar work presented with a very decorative cover in an attempt to suggest that the student spent a lot of time on the work. Most colleges do not allow work to be presented with more than a title page, and students need to get used to being graded on the content of the work and not on how it is displayed.

(Continued)

(Continued)

✓ Make sure that the rules in your class are very clear—posting them can help. At the beginning of the year, go over each rule and the reason for it. This will help later if a student claims not to understand a rule or that it is not "fair."

o For classes with younger students, the rules can be decided by having a guided discussion about what behavior helps the class to run well and respect all the members of the class.

o For classes with older students, rules can be determined by all the students in the class. In that case, post the rules and have each student sign the rules as an indication that she or he agrees to follow the rules. You can have a signed set of rules for each of your classes.

LEARNING DISABILITIES

There is no question that fewer girls are identified with learning disabilities than boys. Most learning disabilities involve language deficits, so it makes sense that the group whose language skills develop sooner are likely to have fewer problems. However, that does not mean that girls do not have learning disabilities, so if a student is not doing well in your class, the reason may be because of learning disabilities.

Children develop different skills at different rates, and schools should be sensitive to those differences. Do remember that what looks like a learning disability may actually be a difference in learning modality or difference in development. Those differences will still need to be addressed, but can be ameliorated by time or differences in teaching and approach.

Dyslexia

Dyslexia is any one of several different difficulties with language, and generally girls are diagnosed with such problems less often than boys. This group of disorders may involve problems with oral language, reading, or written language, and most individuals can learn, but usually in a way that is not typical in classroom instruction (Carreker, 2004). In light of the female verbal advantage, girls with dyslexia may be particularly sensitive to their learning problems because of the assumption that girls are not supposed to have trouble in this area.

The important factor here is to make sure the student is properly identified and receives the correct accommodations for her individual learning issues. Working with the special education teacher assigned to the child will help provide a learning environment where the student can thrive. You might help the child discover what she does know and figure out what means she used to acquire that information. Then assist the student to frame her schoolwork using similar methods. It is crucial to get the student to understand that she does learn, but perhaps the best way for her to learn is not the same way as most of the class. There are many ways to provide accommodations for the child with verbal learning issues, and the special education department at your school is the best source for help with specific strategies for each child.

SUGGESTIONS FOR APPLYING THE THEORY TO YOUR CLASSROOM

✓ For a girl in middle school for whom peer approval is important, being different may mean that that she is reluctant to be identified or singled out as having learning differences. Some girls may be embarrassed if others find out about their learning issues, and some students simply don't care. The problem is that accommodations may unmask her as learning disabled and that may be the reason she will not use the accommodations or allow you to do so.

✓ Very young girls may not be identified yet, so just because a student is not categorized as having dyslexia does not mean that she doesn't have it. One of my students with severe dyslexia was not identified until fourth grade because her spoken verbal skills were so good that it was hard to determine that her academic problems stemmed from her inability to read.

✓ Older students may find some support in talking to a senior female student or adult who has similar problems. Knowing that others have similar problems and have dealt successfully with them can be a great comfort.

✓ Many very prominent individuals are dyslexic. Have a girl do a report on such an individual paying particular attention to how that individual has coped with his or her learning difficulty.

Dysgraphia/Dyspraxia

Although the child with dyslexia has trouble getting information in, the child with dysgraphia has trouble producing information, particularly in writing. Dyspraxia is a more general term indicating difficulties with motor skills and coordination, including handwriting. Either diagnosis will mean that the child has trouble producing written work. The primary identifying characteristic of dysgraphia is poor handwriting, but the problem is far more complicated than that. Again, this is a problem where boys have more trouble, probably because of the combination of slower language skills together with later acquisition of fine motor skills. The child with dysgraphia will have trouble organizing thoughts on paper, will have a large gap between ideas communicated orally and written, will have difficulties with spelling and grammar, and will tire swiftly when writing (Dysgraphia, 2007). People with this problem will have trouble coordinating their hands to do different things at the same time, so playing the piano or a similar two-handed instrument will be difficult.

As a person with severe dysgraphia, I can attest to how much help the computer can be for children with this disorder. Although I tire quickly when writing anything by hand, I can type easily and rapidly, even though I have to say out loud what I am typing as I do so, which is why what I write sounds like I am talking to you. I had serious problems completing English compositions in school, but my son, who has the same problem, was started on a computer in the fourth grade and has far fewer problems. The important thing is to start accommodations early. Girls with dysgraphia should know that there might be a limit to how neat their handwriting can be, and they should be encouraged to use the computer. On the other hand, all children should be required to produce work that is at their level of neatness.

The move to make sure that all children are proficient on the computer may create some problems in the future. Research indicates that recognition of letters and characters, a skill necessary for reading, is promoted if the individual writes the letters as they are being learned (Longcamp et al., 2008; Longcamp, Boucard, Gilhodes, & Velay, 2006). Further, as all teachers know, handwriting has been shown to be an excellent way to learn vocabulary or other material (Naka, 1998). So even if typing is easier for me, I learned long ago that the best way for me to learn anything is to write it over and over, even in my bad handwriting. On the other hand, for writing original work such as essays or books, the computer is my friend.

SUGGESTIONS FOR APPLYING THE THEORY TO YOUR CLASSROOM

✓ Handwriting is not a popular topic to teach, although most small children like the repetitive exercises. Encourage your school or school system to make sure that handwriting is taught to all students.

✓ Make sure that students who have been identified with dysgraphia have ample opportunities to become familiar with the computer as that will assist them in producing neater work. The earlier the student can be properly identified, the more she can use technology to compensate for her difficulties in producing written work.

✓ Even though the student may use the computer to complete long assignments, all students should develop sufficient handwriting skills to write short notes or take down assignments. The new tablet computers provide great assistance for most students in taking notes, and mine has learned to read most of my handwriting!

✓ Girls with dysgraphia need help learning to structure essays using outlines or some other framework that will help them keep on track. Lab reports that have set formats are usually easier for them to complete. What is important is that the student understands that she will write better when she has a concrete structure to focus her efforts.

Dyscalculia

Dyscalculia is the "dys" of math. Although dyslexia and dysgraphia are more common in boys, dyscalculia affects girls and boys equally. Fairly recent information points to memory, specifically working memory, as the source of the problem (Kaufmann, Lochy, Drexler, & Semenza, 2004). Other models suggest that neuropsychological factors other than memory are the cause (Shalev, 2004). The problem is that because no one cause has been identified, treatments deal with symptoms rather than the root of the disorder. One of the most frustrating scenarios of teaching a child with dyscalculia occurs when the teacher spends a lot of one-on-one time to teach the child a specific skill in math and the child seems to master it. The next day, however, the child comes back to class with little or no memory of how to solve similar problems. When the disorder is seen as a specific memory issue or a neurological processing problem and not one of comprehension, it is easier to understand that the difficulty that the dyscalculic has with math can be managed.

I am competent in fairly complicated mathematics and have taught classes from pre-algebra to trigonometry. Yet I cannot calculate the tip for a waitress in my head. Yes, I can move the decimal over to take ten percent of the total; the problem comes when I cannot add two ten percents and the original amount without writing down the numbers. The best feature of my cell phone is the tip calculator! Knowing that my problem in math is a matter of memory makes a huge difference in my confidence that I can manage numbers. After years of making subtraction mistakes, I now justify my checkbook with a calculator. Helping a girl realize that her problem in math may be based on a memory deficit or a processing problem rather than an inability to understand the process may help her be more willing to keep working in math.

SUGGESTIONS FOR APPLYING THE THEORY TO YOUR CLASSROOM

✓ Some help is available at www.ldonline.org. That Web site will assist you in providing methods for your student with dyscalculia to manage her problems in math.

✓ The sooner students' problems in math can be attributed to dyscalculia, the sooner they can begin to use methods to compensate. I've counted on my fingers all my life and I have a calculator with me all the time. All students need to learn the basic facts of math and good retrieval of information from the multiplication tables will help students move more quickly through solving a problem.

✓ A chronic problem for the dyscalculic is reversal of numbers as problems are transferred from a source to a page where the work is to be done. You will give

(Continued)

(Continued)

students hope that they can do math if you will give part credit for those problems if the work is correct although the problem was written down wrong.

✓ A common accommodation is to allow the older dyscalculic students to bring formulas and other similar information to a test for math and science. One way for older students to do this is to program a graphing calculator with that information. Knowing that they don't have to remember those formulas will help the dyscalculic focus on doing the math rather than trying to remember the formulas.

SYNTHESIZING VERSUS ANALYZING

The female brain has been described as the synthesizing brain and the male brain as the analyzing brain (Baron-Cohen, 2003). Simon Baron-Cohen has described the different approaches by pointing out that "the female brain is predominantly hardwired for empathy. The male brain is predominantly hardwired for understanding and building systems" (p. 1). In the classroom, this means that girls need to see the whole picture and boys may be inclined to see the parts. In presenting material to girls, the effective teacher may start by giving the students an overview such as, "Let's look at the table of contents and see where our book is going to take us this year."

Don't forget, some of the girls in your class will have an analyzing approach and some of the boys will have a synthesizing approach to learning. That means that you need to provide both approaches whether or not your class is coed.

SUGGESTIONS FOR APPLYING THE THEORY TO YOUR CLASSROOM

✓ Girls tend to take a very personal approach to learning, which can be very effective as we all find information easier to learn as it applies to us. However, anything you can do to help them objectify what they learn, even in a small way, will help girls understand how anything is put together.

o Encourage young girls to work with building blocks. Generally the boys tend to monopolize those toys, so put some aside for girls to work with. Have them build a dollhouse or a scale model of the classroom.

o Have students use tiles to follow pictures of patterns. Mosaics are an excellent way to build a whole picture by focusing on the details.

✓ If girls tend to look at the big picture, you may need to help them see the building blocks.

    ○ With young students, have them draw the steps in the water cycle. Then have them cut the steps apart. Have them draw a picture of the earth with clouds above and then put the pieces of the water cycle in the correct places.

    ○ In science, older students might understand the basic functions that are performed by a cell, but not be sure of exactly which organelles are responsible for those functions and exactly what is happening. Have the students draw a picture of each organelle down the side of a page and then write the specific function next to the picture. Organelles that work together to perform a function could be color-coded to make them stand together.

LEARNING DIFFERENCES AND THE CLASSROOM

When we learn material, each of us approaches that learning opportunity from the way that makes the most sense to us. That viewpoint is probably shared by many others, but not by all. In the teaching process, if the teacher and learner do not share similar approaches to the material, it may be difficult for the learner to understand what is being taught. It is important for teachers to present information using different learning approaches to maximize the impact that the material has on the students in the class.

In Chapter 8, you will find a brief assessment to determine the preferred learning modalities for your students. They may be interested in finding out this information and learning how best to frame their study approaches.

ANSWERS TO QUIZ

1. B—Boys are more likely to be identified as generally learning disabled, especially true for language-based disabilities. Recent information indicates that such identification may not reflect a teacher bias but indicates that boys have more learning disabilities than girls (Linderman, Kantrowitz, & Flannery, 2005).

2. C—There is no gender difference in dyscalculia, the learning disability in math. There is an equal chance for a girl or a boy to suffer from this disorder (Lachance & Mazzocco, 2006).

3. A—Girls, ages 5 to 17, are better at planning or defining a problem and selecting the appropriate strategy than their male peers (Naglieri & Rojahn, 2001).

(Continued)

(Continued)

4. A—Girls spend more time studying and doing homework after school. Boys are much more likely to be engaged in sports and play both indoors and outdoors (Du, Weymouth, & Dragseth, 2003; National Center for Educational Statistics [NCES], 2007a).

5. B—Boys are very peer oriented and learn better in a collegial atmosphere with other boys than with their teacher (Honigsfeld & Dunn, 2003; Pyryt, Sandals, & Begoray, 1998).

6. B—Boys, even though they learn best in groups, their groups are frequently not academically oriented (Van Houtte, 2004).

7. A—Girls have better proofreading skills. This is related to the skill of perceptual speed and women are faster at comparing symbols and designs (Kimura, 2000; Naglieri & Rojahn, 2001).

8. A—Girls are more willing to check for errors and correct mistakes. Perceptual speed is involved here, but the willingness to do this may be a factor of girls being less impulsive or wanting to be successful (Stumpf, 1998).

9. B—Boys will continue to use familiar strategies even if the method is not successful (Stumpf, 1998).

10. A—Girls are convinced that academic success is tied to the effort expended, but they are better able to be realistic about their progress (Tibbetts, 1977).

3

Dealing With Stress

SOURCE: Photographer: Duane Berger. Used with permission.

I wish I had known the information presented in this chapter earlier in my teaching career, as I taught many girls who suffered from various forms of test and math anxiety. What I have learned fairly recently about differences in the way stress is manifested in females and males has given me some strategies to pass on. My students tell me these strategies work. Is stress a major problem for girls? How stressed are they? See how well you know the facts.

According to the Centers for Disease Control's (CDC) *Youth Risk Behavior Survey* (2008), are girls or boys more likely to engage in the following stressful activities?

QUIZ

Respond to the following statements by indicating whether the statement best describes (a) girls or (b) boys.

1. Do not get at least eight hours of sleep a night

2. Are more likely to control weight by starving or by using bulimic techniques

3. Do not attend physical education classes or belong to a sports team

4. Are more likely to consider suicide or actually attempt suicide

5. May react to stressful situations by freezing

Answers are on page 64.

STRESS

The body's reaction to stress, termed fight-or-flight, has long been understood, and the reaction is the same whether the stressful event is a real one (an impending automobile crash) or an emotional one (a final exam). As the body prepares for the distressful event, it releases adrenaline that results in the sympathetic nervous system response of

- increased heart rate,
- increased blood pressure,
- increased respiration rate,
- increased blood sugar,
- dilated pupils,
- increased blood flow to muscles (away from the skin), and
- gastrointestinal system stops functioning properly.

This response is designed to prepare the individual to fight the impending danger or to run away from it by providing energy for muscles to work. If the stressful event is not very obvious or of brief duration, such as a pop quiz, we may not even be aware that our bodies are reacting this way. If we are under chronic stress, even if that stress is not very obvious to us, the cumulative effect on our bodies can be devastating. It is now known that even small amounts of ongoing stress can affect our immune system, making us more susceptible to all sorts of illnesses including the common cold (Wein, 2000). However, we also require stress so that we can be alert to deal with events in our life, and some stress can actually be beneficial. It is clear that the more we feel in control of a situation, the more we are able to deal successfully with the stress in our lives.

Recently, it has been found that, in some cases, women do not react with the fight-or-flight response. It has been suggested that in women the opposite reaction occurs, a response termed tend-and-befriend. When women are stressed, their bodies produce hormones other than adrenaline, which results in the body becoming quieter and less responsive (Taylor et al., 2000; Turton & Campbell, 2005). According to this theory, the reason females respond differently to stress than males is that if female animals and early female humans ran at the sign of an intruder, it would leave infants behind and put them in jeopardy. If the female was to protect off-spring, then the best response was to become quiet and still to protect the young. One of the hormones involved in this response is oxytocin, a hormone that is released during sexual activity and childbirth.

If a student is stressed by a test and goes through fight-or-flight, that student may find it difficult to write clearly as the muscles are prepared for larger tasks, but blood is in the brain, and the student will be able to think. In this case, a student may find it difficult to control fine-motor movements resulting in poor handwriting. Students may press hard on the paper resulting in *etched* writing or, if using a pencil, the frequent need to resharpen the point. If the student in fight-or-flight has trouble with the test, the student may get upset and express that response by some physical means such as yelling, throwing paper or books, or running out of the classroom.

On the other hand, the student responding to the stress of a test through tend-and-befriend will get very quiet, turn pale, be unable to think, and may become nauseated or cry. The problem is that the blood, instead of going out to the extremities as it does in fight-or-flight, goes to the core of the body, and when this happens, the student cannot move, cannot think, and may become nauseated. To understand the reaction, look at the bodily reactions listed earlier for fight-or-flight and think of the opposite reactions. So if heart rate increases for fight-or-flight stress response, heart rate decreases for tend-and-befriend stress response. When I describe this reaction in class, many of my female students will grin, but agree that it is true. Of course, this is not true for all females or true every time a female takes a test, but it is one important factor in the development of test anxiety in females.

One of the biggest problems with test anxiety is anticipation of the response. Learning theory tells us that if our bodies have responded to a situation with one of the stress reactions, we are likely to respond similarly the next time simply because we are used to it. Students may predict that they will have trouble with a test because they *know* that they will have a stress reaction. Helping students change their expectations of problems with tests is crucial to helping them learn to deal successfully with the test experience. As I tell my students,

> You weren't afraid of tests the first time you took one; you learned to be anxious, and you can unlearn that response. The problem is that it took some time to become very test anxious, and you won't get over that feeling quickly. What we hope is that you will learn some strategies to help you feel optimistic about your future success in dealing with test anxiety.

Watch girls when they come out of high-stakes tests; they crowd around one another talking about how nervous they were and supporting one another. Boys, on the other hand, when stressed, get restless and physical, but they can think. After a stressful test, they will go to the basketball court and shoot hoops. That doesn't mean that boys won't talk about the experience later, they will, but right after a stressful test, they need to do something physical because of their fight-or-flight stress response. While their physical response helps boys in stressful situations, it can hinder girls.

Once you recognize that one of your female students suffers from test anxiety because of a tend-and-befriend response, make sure that she is aware that the response is an automatic one and quite normal. I have found that girls may believe that they are the only person who responds in this manner and knowing that there are other sufferers will help defuse the feeling of impending doom. Knowing that the response is a normal reaction to stress and is not necessarily linked to a particular situation may also help a student feel encouraged that she will be able to control how she reacts to the testing situation.

MANAGEMENT OF TEST ANXIETY

Test anxiety occurs when a student has a stress reaction to a testing situation. Whether the stress reaction takes the form of fight-or-flight or tend-and-befriend, the response occurs to help us cope with stressful or dangerous situations especially if the situation is a physical or an emotional danger. If the body responds with fight-or-flight, the symptoms are obvious to the individual as the heart starts to beat rapidly, the respiratory rate increases, and the individual is aware of being more alert to her surroundings. If the body responds with tend-and-befriend, the reaction is more subtle and the individual may not be aware that she is responding this way until she is unable to think well or to move. If you were in a car accident, either reaction would be considered normal and you would probably be directed to sit down and take it easy. If you have the same reaction in a test, you may be told that you have test anxiety and you shouldn't be afraid of a test. We may have learned to be afraid of tests at some point in the past and it is not easy to unlearn that reaction just because we want to.

SUGGESTIONS FOR APPLYING THE THEORY TO YOUR CLASSROOM

✓ Young girls may not yet respond to tests with tend-and-befriend, but they do need to learn that tests do not have to be stressful. Take a few minutes before a test to talk generally about the test, encouraging students to engage in positive self-talk. Help them put each test in perspective and understand that tests are not a major hurdle to success but a step on the ladder to knowledge.

✓ Help girls who suffer from test anxiety realize that it is a physiological response to stress and that there are ways that they can control their response. The most important thing is for girls to understand that they are in control of their lives and their bodies. This lesson is important on so many different levels, but this is a great place to start. Remember, the more control a student believes she has over what is happening, the less stress she feels.

✓ Make sure that girls know that not everyone is anxious about tests. What happens is that in the midst of a stress reaction, girls may generalize and believe that test anxiety is universal. Knowing that it is possible to take a test and not get anxious can be comforting.

In helping girls deal with test anxiety, the first step is to identify a child's reaction as test anxiety, as not all children will exhibit the same symptoms. If the child responds with fight-or-flight, the reaction is usually easy to detect as the child's activity increases. If the child enters tend-and-befriend, the symptoms are very different. The problem is that it is difficult to determine if a girl is in this state, as she will be very quiet, although crying is not an unusual response to serious stress. However, the usual tip-off is if she says she feels sick, or she tells you that she couldn't remember the material and you believe that she knows the answers.

Test anxiety is a chronic problem for girls in math and it starts early. Many of my students at all levels have told me that they don't ever remember not being scared of math tests. After watching my test-anxious students, the answer is pretty clear that a major part of the problem is the tend-and-befriend response (Taylor et al., 2000). For girls, the key is the inability to retrieve information when stressed. They become quiet and upset and the more upset they become, the less they can remember. Once they leave the testing situation, the stress lessens, blood flow returns to normal, they remember the answers, and they can communicate how frustrating it is to forget well-known material in a testing situation.

The solution is simple. Get the blood flowing to the extremities; if the heart is pumping blood to the arms and legs, the blood is going to the brain as well. However, even though you encourage a girl to move around, she may be so upset that it is difficult for her to do so.

SUGGESTIONS FOR APPLYING THE THEORY TO YOUR CLASSROOM

✓ Make sure that the student understands that she is still responsible and that test anxiety is not an excuse for failing to complete the test.

✓ The student should learn to identify the symptoms that indicate that she is going to have an attack of test anxiety so that she can take steps to reduce the effect of stress. One of the first principles of stress management is to begin treatment very early. You and she need a signal so that she can indicate to you that she is feeling stressed.

✓ The student should go out of the classroom or testing area and walk around or should have some plan to increase her heart rate. Be careful, if the student has allowed the situation to progress too far, she may feel faint if she stands up.

✓ Encourage her to take control of the problem and not become a victim to her body's response to stress. Practice positive self-talk and other methods to calm her anxiety. The more she realizes that she can control this response, she is more likely to be able to do so.

✓ Yoga is a wonderful means for individuals to become aware of their bodily responses and by using breathing techniques, control the body's responses. For the older student, learning yoga will help. Some coaches are familiar with helping students learn to focus by slowing their breathing, and the technique is much the same as yoga breathing.

✓ Seek counseling or therapy if she is unable to control the symptoms or the symptoms begin to affect aspects of school other than tests.

Do not spring this on a student. If you are going to recommend this, work with the school counselor and the girl to prepare a plan for her to begin to learn to manage her own anxiety. The stress response is an automatic reaction of our bodies. Once we are faced with a stressful situation, it seems as if there is no way to control what happens. If you suspect that a child has test anxiety, check with the school counselor to see what the school policy is on management of test anxiety. Some counselors are trained to teach children relaxation techniques or may know of local professionals who are qualified. As the teacher of a test anxious child, you can help by

- identifying test anxious children to parents and to the appropriate school services,
- offering alternative testing methods and sites to reduce anxiety so that students can learn to manage their responses to the testing situation,
- encouraging students to use relaxation techniques appropriately, and
- providing a class atmosphere where students feel comfortable coming for help.

You will find some hints on how to help girls learn to answer test questions in Chapter 8.

Math Anxiety

A special form of test anxiety is math anxiety. I've had students do badly on all kinds of tests and stomp out of the room after tossing the test on my desk with a parting remark to the effect that I needn't bother grading the test as they failed it. I've had students who told me before exams that they were really worried that they were going to do badly, and they were correct. But the only students I have had who appear to work diligently while taking a math test and then turn in the test having only answered a few questions were girls. When I asked these students why they didn't answer more questions, the reply was, "I just couldn't remember how to solve the problems."

While test anxiety will make it very difficult for a student to perform well in any testing situation, math anxiety may interfere with a student's ability to learn that particular subject at all. I remember being in French class, a course that I failed to pass numerous times, and thinking that if I thought something was the answer, it must not be right because every answer I came up with was wrong. I had a sinking feeling in the pit of my stomach every day until French class was over, as just being in class was totally humiliating. At least part of my problem in learning French was my fear of the subject. When I share that feeling with girls in my math classes, some of them will give me a nod of agreement, as they know exactly what I am talking about. If a girl develops math anxiety, it will start early and may continue to grow throughout her life if there is no intervention. The problem is that the girl worries both about her ability to do well in math as well as how badly she perceives she is doing (Wigfield & Meece, 1988). Remember, this is different from test anxiety, as the student with math anxiety is worried about her ability to learn math; the student with test anxiety knows she understands the material, but she has trouble with the pressure of the test situation.

SUGGESTIONS FOR APPLYING THE THEORY TO YOUR CLASSROOM

✓ Be alert for statements by young students that indicate that they have some fear associated with math. No matter how often you show these students how well they are doing, they will continue to think otherwise. One way to deal with this is to give small tests three or four times a week. The tests don't have to be long, three or four questions will do, but part of the problem with test anxiety is anticipation, and with frequent tests, there is less time to ruminate.

✓ Give students tests to take home. If you do that, allow them to use any information they can find to answer the questions, and that includes asking friends and relations. The best kinds of questions are those that use math in a practical situation. This will help students understand that they can do math.

✓ It is very important that a girl knows the difference between test anxiety and math anxiety, as it is easy to confuse the two. The student who is test anxious has troubles in all courses and it may be easier to work on developing skills to manage her stress in another course. The student who is math anxious needs to know that it is not the testing situation that causes her problems but the subject. It is quite possible that she will confuse the two and decide that she is test anxious. The problem is that believing she is test anxious will affect all of her courses not just math.

✓ Organize a study group of girls who aren't doing well. Help them focus on what they do well and how they can support one another rather than centering on their math shortcomings. Success should be judged by improvement not by reaching some arbitrary grade. Here older students can serve as peer models for doing well in math.

  o These students can have review sessions before tests.
  o These students can work on stress management techniques together.
  o These students can have celebratory gatherings after a test (make sure that they are focusing on successes and not on perceived failures).

ABILITY VERSUS EFFORT

Earlier, we covered the idea that one difference between girls and boys in class is their attitude toward what they believe is responsible for academic success. Both teachers and students believe that girls succeed because they work hard and boys succeed because they are academically capable (Epstein, 1999; Fennema, Peterson, Carpenter, & Lubinski, 1990). Combine the attitude that effort is necessary to succeed in school with the internal-stress-management pattern typical of tend-and-befriend, and it is not surprising that girls worry about their performance more than boys (Pomerantz et al., 2002). Additionally, because girls are predisposed to please adults, they believe that failure to succeed also fails the adults (Pomerantz & Ruble, 1998), and that adds even more pressure to do well.

Girls direct their energies to mastery of material, whereas boys are more concerned with performance (Kenney-Benson, Pomerantz, Ryan, & Patrick, 2006). This may mean that girls want to make sure that they really understand the material and boys are only interested in the grade they get on the test, in spite of the fact that the girls are usually doing better. This focus on mastery has been given as one reason girls are less disruptive in class because they believe that mastery requires sustained effort (Kenney-Benson et al.). Another part of this picture is the finding that women view academic evaluation as an opportunity to assess their abilities, which can lead to more stress if they see a drop in performance.

Because girls believe so strongly in the benefit of effort, they are more willing than boys to work hard and do what they are told. One study replicating the findings that girls get better grades in school, whereas boys get better grades on standardized tests, found that one reason for the difference was the emphasis on self-discipline by the girls (Duckworth & Seligman, 2006). This study was conducted in a middle school, and the question was posed whether the stronger female academic self-discipline would persist into high school. Having taught girls in both middle and high school, I have noticed that a conscientious work ethic does persist for many girls, especially if they believe that harder work will pay off. Some of my students who had trouble in class, especially in math, gave up as soon as they perceived that they did not understand what they were asked to do. They believed that no amount of effort would help them.

On the other hand, the problem with this emphasis on effort is that if a girl is having trouble in a class, her first response may be to work harder. What happens is that the time spent on the class she is having trouble with may take away from the amount of time allotted to the rest of her work. I have seen girls get so focused with what amounts to an obsession to do well in a class that they lose all perspective. These students may fail other classes, become so stressed that they end up with various illnesses, or develop depression because they believe that they cannot improve. One student told me that there was no hope for her and she was going to fail for the year. When I questioned her, she said that she put all her free time and more into studying her math and still couldn't do better than a C, and now the amount of time she spent on math was beginning to show as the grades in her other classes were dropping from As to Bs. We had a long talk about how having straight As in all of her courses except for a C in math was still going to get her into the college of her choice, as she wanted to major in creative writing.

SUGGESTIONS FOR APPLYING THE THEORY TO YOUR CLASSROOM

✓ Provide rubrics so that your students will know exactly what level of work will meet the standards for success. That will help the student who is focused on effort know when she has met criteria.

  o For very young students, a rubric may be a simple checklist of items or information that is to be included in the final product.
  o Older students will need to have a more extensive description of what constitutes a successful completion of the task together with an understanding of the criteria to determine whether the product meets expectations.

✓ Stress can be exacerbated by a need to find the *right* answer. This is another reason to give students practice developing alternative solutions or paths to solve problems.

✓ When a student asks what material will be on the test or asks you to provide an outline of the material for a test, resist falling into that trap. The problem is that the student is only focusing on the test and not on larger concepts. One way is to ask students of all ages to provide questions they think would be appropriate for the material. For older students, you can divide the class into study groups and assign one chapter to each group to provide an outline.

✓ For the girl who is so focused on how she is doing that it obscures everything else, help her develop a way to keep track of her grades and show her how to estimate how she is doing. One of the major problems is that these girls will concentrate on their shortcomings and not notice where they are doing well. She needs to realize that one bad grade will not ruin her average, and by looking at all her grades and not just the bad ones, she will have a better perspective on her progress in the course.

Self-Handicapping

Have you ever gone out to a party the night before a big exam telling yourself that this will help you relax so you will do better? And if you don't do better, well then, how could you expect to perform well because you partied the night before. That is called self-handicapping and is the practice of making plans for activities that will interfere with successful performance and on which the failure can be blamed. This is a way to deal with stress by not admitting the stress is there. The general belief is that boys self-handicap more than girls and most research bears that out (Hirt, McCrea, & Boris, 2003; Lucas & Lovaglia, 2005).

Although self-handicapping is generally described as a behavior that can be used as an excuse for lack of success, other situations not traditionally thought of as self-handicapping can arise to interfere with success. Having taught math to girls, I have seen a host of self-handicapping strategies, such as the perceived need to study other subjects to the point where there is no time left for math. Other strategies with similar results involve helping a friend who is having an emotional crisis, having an emotional crisis of your own, being unable to cope with the problems of doing poorly in a subject, and simply deciding (with no real evidence) that you are no good at math and, therefore, cannot possibly do well so there is no reason to study. One report agreed and found that girls self-handicapped more than boys when emotional and cognitive issues were included (Warner & Moore, 2004).

SUGGESTIONS FOR APPLYING THE THEORY TO YOUR CLASSROOM

✓ Girls who are extremely competitive with themselves should be aware of the problems that can arise if they discover they are never satisfied with their performance. The issue is one of stress management, and focusing on how they are doing may simply be a way to direct the attention away from the real problem—that they lack confidence in math or science:

  o Stress management is essential for many areas, but for some girls it can make the difference between failing and doing very well in math.

  o If you have a number of students who are math anxious or who engage in what you believe to be self-handicapping behaviors, work with the school counselor to develop a group to deal with the anxiety. Girls frequently believe that no one else can possibly get as anxious about a math test as they can, and being able to talk about their problems with fellow sufferers will help them understand that the reaction is normal. The group might practice yoga breathing techniques, aerobic exercise, or other methods to assist in managing stress.

✓ For students in the middle school grades, public acknowledgment of failure is difficult. Knowing that others also have troubles might help, but it also might convince a girl that she is a total loser in math. Developing confidence at this age is something that may best happen in a one-on-one situation. High school students who need community service hours are an excellent group from which to draw slightly older mentors with a better perspective on doing well in a subject.

✓ If the problem is self-handicapping, the first step is to face the student with the fact that the behavior is interfering with her ability to do well in the course. The student may have a hard time admitting that helping her friend in an emotional crisis is simply a way to get out of doing her own studying. If you are not comfortable helping a student with the following steps, ask the school counselor for assistance. I have had some success getting girls to examine their behavior in this way:

  o First, admit that the behavior is self-handicapping.
  o Second, face the belief that drives the self-handicapping behavior.
  o Third, collect evidence that disproves the belief.
  o Fourth, acknowledge that the skills are there or can be learned.
  o Fifth, plan new patterns of behavior.

Stereotype Threat

When you believe that you are hopeless at some task simply because of your group membership, that is called stereotype threat, and it is a special form of self-handicapping. The idea is that the individual believes the stereotype because they belong to the group, and they do not work because of the conviction that failure is almost certain (Keller, 2002; Spencer, Steele, & Quinn, 1999). Research is very clear that some women do poorly in math simply because they believe the notion that women don't do well in math. Telling a group of women that a math problem is particularly hard for women will result in lower scores than if a similar group of women was not told that the problem was difficult (Huguet & Régner, 2007). Although science does not have the reputation for being as hard for women as math, there is an indication that stereotype threat can affect a woman's scores on tests in that discipline as well (Andre, Whigham, Hendrickson, & Chambers, 1999; Breakwell, Vignoles, & Robertson, 2003).

One way to help girls deal with this problem is simply to tell them about it. Point out that females may do poorly in math simply because they believe that they will. When females are told that they are as competent in math as males, the result is an improvement in females' grades on math tests (Johns, Schmader, & Martens, 2005; Lesko & Corpus, 2006). Another method that has worked to improve girls' grades in math is to let them take a test by themselves or in a room with other girls (Johns et al., 2005). That will not be possible for state standard exams, but if it is possible for you to do on your tests, let girls have the experience of taking a test in a single-sex environment. If your students realize that it is the situation that is the problem and not the subject matter, you may be able to convince them that they can do better on math tests.

FOCUS

Students who suffer from test anxiety or other stress reactions may find it difficult to focus on what is happening in class. When the student acquires strategies to manage her stress reactions, she will find it easier to concentrate on the lesson. However, stress is not the only reason students may find it difficult to focus in class.

Generally, students who are identified with problems of focus or attention tend to be boys. However, girls suffer from attention deficit/hyperactivity disorder (ADHD) as well. Over time, the hyperactive symptoms in some girls will ameliorate, but in others, the inattentive symptoms remained after five years, even though those students were likely to have fewer other problems (Hinshaw, Owens, Sami, & Fargeon, 2006). This same study reported that the one area where girls diagnosed with both hyperactive and inattentive symptoms, what is known as ADHD–combined type, did not make progress in was mathematics.

It is possible that some of these students did not actually suffer from ADHD. Many of the girls identified with ADHD–inattentive type did not have the same pattern of disability as the students who were only hyperactive or who had the combined type (Hinshaw et al., 2006). There is a school of thought that believes that many students who are identified with ADHD do not have the disorder (Armstrong, 1996; James, 2007). For example, I have a lot of energy and am somewhat restless, especially if I have to sit for a long period. Combine that with my poor auditory memory and I look a lot like a person with ADHD. However, I will be able to tell you every detail of what happened so I don't lack attention, and I can focus for long periods on active tasks such as writing. Children who cannot tell the teacher what was just said in class can be accused of not paying attention when the problem may involve some entirely different issue.

Certainly girls do suffer from ADHD. However, when girls with ADHD are identified, they seem to be more affected by the condition than the average boy with ADHD (Gaub & Carlson, 1997; Rucklidge & Tannock, 2001). The theory is that because girls are less active to begin with, by the time a student is disabled enough to come to the attention of the teacher, the student will have serious problems. Girls with ADHD-inattentive type may slip through the cracks, as their impairment is probably not as noticeable as that of boys with similar levels of inattention. If a girl is having trouble in your class, do not dismiss ADHD as the cause just because she is not as obviously hyperactive as most of the identified boys. On the other hand, make sure that the problem lies in attentional issues and not in other issues that may affect a child's ability to remember class information.

SUGGESTIONS FOR APPLYING THE THEORY TO YOUR CLASSROOM

✓ If a child appears to be daydreaming and cannot always repeat what was just said in class, the problem may be ADHD-inattention or some other issue.

○ Put the child in a different place in class. It is possible that she cannot see the board and being closer to the teacher will help a child focus.

○ As you say directions, give the child you are concerned with a copy of written directions. A child with ADHD will not get all the information from either source, but if the child has an auditory-processing problem, giving her written directions will help.

✓ Document what is going on in the class when the child seems the most inattentive and what happens in class that holds her attention. This information will provide data for the special education teacher in making a determination of attentional issues.

MANAGEMENT OF DISTRACTIONS

The usual belief is that girls are less susceptible to distraction in the classroom and are, therefore, better able to concentrate. The problem is that distractions for girls frequently come from within and are, therefore, much harder to identify and, even if identified, harder to help girls deal with. When both teacher and student understand the process, it is much easier for students to acquire methods to help them manage their distractions.

ANSWERS TO QUIZ

1. A—71% of girls fail to get enough sleep whereas 67% of boys admit to poor sleep habits (CDC, 2008).

2. A—6.4% of girls admit to unhealthy weight control, whereas only 2.2% of boys do (CDC, 2008).

3. A—50% of girls do not attend PE classes, whereas 42% of boys do not have regular physical education; 50% of girls belong to a sports team, whereas 72% of boys belong to a team (CDC, 2008).

4. A—18.7% of girls admit that they have seriously considered suicide whereas 10% of boys admit to that. 9.3% of girls have actually made a serious suicide attempt; only 4.6% of boys have done so. Suicide is the third leading cause of death for adolescents (CDC, 2008).

5. A—Girls may react to stressful situations by freezing. Boys respond to stress with fight-or-flight, but girls may respond with what is termed tend-and-befriend behavior (Taylor et al., 2000).

4

Teaching Math to the Female Brain

One of the major problems with teaching math to girls is that some are still convinced that math is too hard or that they can't learn math. We have already considered that poor spatial skills may be one factor in certain types of math for why girls have difficulty with math. We discovered that another problem might be that girls use words instead of symbols, which are used in mathematics, to access verbal memory when they try to remember material. In this chapter, we will see if these factors are as inflexible a barrier to success in math as popular culture might lead us to believe them to be. There is some concern that girls' verbal-auditory learning style may not be best suited for the typical math classroom, which may favor an iconic-kinesthetic learning style. Overall, however, the reasons girls should not do well in math are not as insurmountable as they might appear. So that raises the question, how well *do* girls do in math? See how many of the following questions you can answer correctly.

QUIZ

Respond to the following statements by indicating whether the statement best describes (a) girls, (b) boys, or (c) both girls and boys.

1. Scored better on the National Association of Educational Progress (NAEP) math and reading tests in 2007

2. Reached or exceeded mathematics proficiency on the 2004 NAEP for eighth graders

3. Reached or exceeded mathematics proficiency on the 2004 NAEP for 12th graders

4. Scored better on the math test on the 2007 SAT

5. Earned more total high school credits in math and science by graduation in 2005

6. Had the highest math and science combined grade point average (GPA) as seniors in 2005

7. Obtained more high school credits in advanced math—Algebra II, pre-calculus, calculus, and advanced-placement (AP) Calculus—in 2000

8. Obtained more bachelor degrees in mathematics in 2004

9. Received more bachelor degrees in 2004, combining all science, mathematics, and engineering (SME) fields

10. Received the fewest number of degrees in engineering in 2004

Answers are on page 88.

When you look at the answers to these questions, you will find that girls are not doing as badly in math as you may have been led to believe. In addition, girls do better on classwork and teacher-made tests but have more trouble with standardized tests (Duckworth & Seligman, 2006). Although girls do not do as well as boys on the standardized mathematics tests, they do much better on standardized tests in reading. It is not clear why this is so, as there are few discussions of this based on recent data and they do not seem to reflect the current school environment—at least as reflected in data from national educational statistics.

PERFORMANCE IN MATH

A major concern, as reflected in research, is that girls opt out of higher-level math classes before they even attempt them (Kimball, 1989; Reid & Roberts, 2006). However, if you look at the statistics cited in the answers to the quiz, you will note that high-school girls take more math classes overall than boys, and more girls take Algebra II and pre-calculus than boys (Snyder, Tan, & Hoffman, 2006). That has not been true for very long, and more boys take calculus and AP calculus than girls. Few students take these advanced classes and the number of girls enrolled in them is growing. It appears that girls' attitudes toward math are changing ever so slowly. The problem remains that they don't do as well on the standardized tests, and in an educational climate where state standard exams are the norm, this is cause for concern.

Another worry is that young girls, particularly those below the sixth grade, still believe that they don't do well in math despite evidence to the contrary (Dickhäuser & Meyer, 2006; Lachance & Mazzocco, 2006). In 2004, fourth-grade girls scored two points lower than boys on the NAEP, in spite of the fact that girls consistently have higher GPAs in math as well as other courses (Shettle et al., 2007). Even with these successes, many girls continue to believe that they are not capable in math (Carr & Davis, 2001). Why do girls who perform well in math do poorly on the standardized tests and believe they can't do math?

Testing Differences

One theory about testing differences is that boys and girls have different learning styles in math and the male style is conducive to doing better on standardized tests. This is not related to test anxiety but to the way that students take tests.

Time

Because of their impulsivity, males are more likely to guess at answers, especially on the multiple-choice items frequently found on standardized tests. Additionally, females are more likely to compare the various choices in a multiple-choice item to their own answers to make sure they have selected correctly (Gallagher & Kaufman, 2005). Because of their cautious approach, females may take more time with each item and, on a standardized test, may not complete as many questions. I point out to my female students that on a multiple-choice test they can make a case for every choice being right. They agree that when they do not immediately recognize the answer, they will examine each choice, sometimes taking a great deal of time when they can't decide on the correct response. You will find suggestions for helping students develop skills with a variety of test styles in Chapter 8.

Most of my female students generally check every answer, whether it is computational or free response, in stark contrast to many of my male students who finish too quickly and don't check their answers. Research supports that observation, noting that although checking reduces incorrect answers, it increases time spent on completing each item (Stumpf, 1998). So part of the problem that some girls have with standardized tests is working too slowly. Don't forget, in 1900, there were few standardized tests, so in comparison to males, females were the stars because they shine on teacher-made tests, which have more generous times for completion.

SUGGESTIONS FOR APPLYING THE THEORY TO YOUR CLASSROOM

✓ If students have trouble with standardized exams, there are a number of approaches you can take to help them. In Chapter 8, you will find some hints on how to help girls learn to answer questions.

o Give one or two sample questions from released versions of standardized exams as pop quizzes several times a week or develop items that follow the format of the exams for your area. Don't make the pop quizzes count a great deal, but they should count some. Repetition will help students get used to taking this type of test.

o Start a study group for students who have trouble with standardized tests. Analyze the questions, plan how to solve certain problem types, and develop strategies for managing panic.

o Help young girls learn to depend more on recall of facts and less on figuring out each solution from the beginning. Practice mental math no matter what level of math students are studying. Yes, I know that girls do not like this method. However, if they develop recall skills in early grades, they will be more willing to use this approach.

o If it is possible, allow girls to take the tests in a room with only other girls, not with boys present. At the very least, talk with your students about why girls may take more time on standardized tests to help them realize their rate is normal and does not indicate that they do not understand math as well as those who complete the tests more rapidly.

Verbal Skills

Students with good verbal skills are likely to use those skills to solve problems. If the best way to solve a math problem doesn't involve verbal skills but rather application of algorithms or use of paradigms, very verbal girls may require a great deal of time to turn the equation into a narrative (Gallagher & Kaufman, 2005). I've had girls come to me in the middle of a test simply asking me to read the question to them so that they can hear the words, as they are having trouble turning the symbols into words for themselves. For example, for the problem $3(2x + 7) = -3$, what a girl may be asking to hear is "three times the quantity of two x plus seven equals negative three."

Another problem here is that if the girl who depends on the words to understand what she is doing uses the wrong words, she may find it hard to rectify her error. Liza was having a great deal of difficulty getting the correct answer to a trigonometry problem we were working on. She kept telling herself that *tangent* was *adjacent side over opposite side*, when it is the other way around. I kept reminding her it was *opposite over adjacent*; she finally figured out that the mnemonic she was using to remember the order was faulty. Liza was using alphabetic order and had *A* for adjacent before *O* for opposite. Even after she found her mistake, every time she faced a problem using tangent, she had to rethink the whole process. She asked me what method I used, and I said that I had just learned that it was *opposite over adjacent*—pure retrieval. Girls want to be sure they have the right answer and may depend on memory aids to help them. Using retrieval devices will maximize their chance for a correct answer, but may increase the time it takes to complete the question.

SUGGESTIONS FOR APPLYING THE THEORY TO YOUR CLASSROOM

✓ With younger students, help them reach automaticity with basic math facts. The younger the girl is, the more likely she will be to trust her answers. Drill on math facts is not the most popular exercise in class, but it will help students solve problems more quickly later on, and there are many ways to make this fun. Look at the Web sites in Chapter 8 for various approaches to math drill.

○ Have the students draw circles divided into regular pie-shaped sections. For younger students, the circles can be divided into eight sections, and for older students, the circles can be divided into 16 sections. Put a small paper clip on the center of the circle, and put the point of a pencil on the center through the paper clip. The student is to spin the clip twice and mark what numbers are indicated by the position of the clip. The student is then to make a fraction with those numbers; reduce the fraction, if possible; and make an improper fraction, a mixed number, and a decimal equivalent, if possible. No calculators are to be used, and students should do this exercise several times in a row with a limited amount of time.

(Continued)

(Continued)

- o Use a domino set to have younger students recognize and match numbers quickly.
- o Have math bees, which are similar to spelling bees—what is 7×5? Reduce the fraction $\frac{6}{8}$. Girls will want to confer with their peers and that will slow them down. If you start testing mental math early in the elementary grades, you can teach girls to rely on themselves.
- o Working in teams may help their confidence. Divide your class into several teams of about four students each. Read a problem and have a buzzer system or flags to indicate when a team has an answer. If this is started early, girls will participate, but you will have to start slowly with older girls who may not have a lot of confidence in their ability to solve problems quickly.
- o Equivalents can be made into a game to play that will help students develop mental-math skills. This can include changing decimals to fractions or percents and back again or finding the metric value of an English measurement. You can use worksheets with some of the data provided and the students are to complete the information or have groups of students working together to solve the problems.
- o Put students in pairs and give each pair four dice. One student will roll all four dice and the other student must add them quickly in her head. The student who is rolling can check with a calculator, but the point is that both will have the chance to do mental math. A pair of dice can be used to work on multiplication skills in the same fashion. If the girls prefer, they can use the spinners to generate numbers.

✓ If an older student needs to translate a math equation to its verbal equivalent, help her learn to do that faster. Much of the difficulty that girls have is being unsure of exactly how to turn the problem into words, and practice will help. Have these students actually write the equations in words as part of their homework.

✓ Keeping a math dictionary in the back of her notebook will give a girl practice turning math into words more easily.

✓ There are math songs to help students learn multiplication tables and other basic math facts. Girls may not realize that they are learning math while they are singing a song.

✓ Above all, make sure that you do not let girls get upset when they have difficulty achieving automaticity with math facts. A sense of humor will greatly help as will having the girls keep a count of how many they get correct each time. This will help them chart their progress.

Competition

We usually don't think of girls as being competitive, but they are very competitive with themselves, termed *indirect competition* or getting a *personal best* (Gallagher, 1998). A timed test can stir up a feeling of competitiveness, and if you are competing with yourself, you can never do well enough. The timed nature of standardized tests contributes to the stress that a girl may already be feeling because of the high stakes involved with doing well. Combine that stress with the female internal stress management style, and indirect competition can lead to a girl being stressed and finding it difficult to think or reason well.

Have girls work together in groups and they can do much better, but only if the climate of the group is cooperative (Gallagher, 1998). Girls tend to be ruminative, they worry, and that trait can interfere with the ability to solve problems quickly and efficiently. The social support of a group may help a girl move on in the problem-solving process rather than obsessing about whether each step is done correctly (Hong, O'Neil, & Feldon, 2005; Keri, 2002). Of course, students need to learn to do work on their own, but introducing material as part of a group exercise may take away some of the pressure. This idea was confirmed by a study where girls performed better on math tests in single-sex groups than in coed groups or alone (Huguet & Régner, 2007).

SUGGESTIONS FOR APPLYING THE THEORY TO YOUR CLASSROOM

✓ Start group work early, letting all students in the early grades work together on problems. Mix the groups up so that the same children do not always work with one another. That will insure that every child has an opportunity to solve problems.

  o Having students work together on simple worksheets will give them practice sharing their strategies.

  o If the desks in your room are arranged in pods, it is easy for students sitting next to one another to work together. Encourage them to do so.

✓ Older students will also benefit from group work. Give problems to groups of students to solve that use principles of the math being studied. Each group should get a different problem and present the solution to the whole class. That method insures that all students will be exposed to a wider range of problems.

✓ You can make a round-robin chart for the class so that every student gets the opportunity to work with every other student. That way, there will be less complaining that a student does not want to work with another.

WHY GIRLS DON'T LIKE MATH

At least part of the problem with girls and math is that many just don't like the subject and others have accepted the notion that girls can't do well in math, so there is no reason for them to try to like it. In teaching girls, I've discovered that I can overcome some of that dislike by introducing the material in ways that appeal to them, but some girls may be hard to convince. Don't be discouraged if you can't turn all of your students into Kovalevskaya clones (Sofia Kovalevskaya, 1850–1891, was a famous Russian mathematician after whom an award for mathematics achievement by a woman is named), but you will have succeeded if you can get them to agree that math is okay and that girls can do well in the subject.

Lack of Confidence

Part of the issue is that middle-school girls are particularly prone to being very sensitive about public failure. This is a factor of a growing self-consciousness in young girls, which is exacerbated by peer pressure, but also by a need to conform to an ideal that the girl believes is necessary to be accepted by others (Apter, 2006; Herbert & Stipek, 2005). Failure of any kind means that the girl does not fit the standard and, in her mind, risks exclusion (Stipek & Gralinski, 1991). She tries to become the ideal model—very stressful if you are not successful.

Much of the research in this area was done some years ago, and at that time the general consensus was that the major problems girls faced in mathematics were that they lacked confidence and believed that math was hard for girls (Hyde, Fennema, & Ryan, 1990; Jones, 1989). More recent work is finding that some girls are changing their minds about math and are much more positive about their ability to do well (Forgasz, Leder, & Kloosterman, 2004; Lloyd, Walsh, & Yailagh, 2005). However, in talking to teachers and to students, it appears that the problem still exists; many girls still believe that math is not for them, and recent findings confirm that lack of confidence in math ability remains a problem for many girls (Frenzel, Pekrun, & Goetz, 2007). Also, the dropping numbers of women obtaining degrees in math are an indication that girls are becoming less interested in math (Snyder et al., 2006).

Lack of Skills

When girls say that they can't *do* math, one area that they point to is their lack of skills in spatial relationships. Earlier, we discussed the three major types: (1) Males performed better than females at tasks involving mental rotation, (2) males perform somewhat better than females at tasks of spatial perception, and (3) males perform equally well as females at tasks of spatial visualization (Linn & Petersen, 1985). More recent information replicates these findings when testing female under-graduates who major in the arts and social sciences. However, under-graduates who major in science, technology, engineering, and math (STEM) courses do not show the same differences (Quaiser-Pohl & Lehmann, 2002). The question is, of course, whether females with better spatial skills choose majors in math and science or whether taking those courses improves their skills, but in any case, there are females with very good spatial skills.

What always amuses me is that many of the women I know tell me that they were simply hopeless in math, particularly in geometry. These same women can go shopping for a piece of furniture without measuring where it is going, and when they get it home, they find it fits perfectly in the room. They can also balance a complicated house-hold budget and keep track of the rising price of milk without any trouble. When I point out that those are fairly complicated math skills, they tell me it is not the same. It is the same, but this points to the solution for many girls—practical application makes math easier to understand.

SUGGESTIONS FOR APPLYING THE THEORY TO YOUR CLASSROOM

✓ Practice with spatial tasks may improve a student's ability. Give students who either have little confidence in their ability with spatial tasks or have demonstrated poor ability exercises to develop facility with spatial skills. Such exercises will include mazes, model building, tangrams, tessellations, origami, prisms, and work with Cuisenaire rods. This training will have the most effect on younger students.

  o Fractals are repeating designs that get smaller and smaller. A computer program to design braided cornrow hairstyles using fractals was developed by Ron Eglash at the Rensselaer Polytechnic Institute. Directions for using Cornrow Curves and many other culturally situated design tools using math can be found on Dr. Eglash's Web site at http://www.rpi.edu/~eglash/csdt.html.

✓ Experts are divided on whether or not spatial skills can be improved. However, if girls are to improve their spatial skills, start as early as possible.

  o Have students draw a scale map of their room, measuring length of walls and space occupied by furniture.
  o Demonstrate how to lay out a pattern on fabric to make a costume for a school play or bags that are designed to contain necessary items to be hung from wheelchairs or walkers. As students get better at this, the fabric can have a pattern that must be taken into account when cutting the pieces out.
  o When making roll-out cookies, try to figure out what is the most efficient placement for the cookie cutters on the dough.
  o Build with blocks, clay, or other materials.
  o Use prisms and other lenses to show how the direction of light changes as it passes through the object. It is easy to trace the path and then measure the angle of deflection. Put a pencil in water in a transparent container, and the pencil appears to bend. That angle of deflection can also be measured.
  o When introducing graphing, start by using geoboards and string instead of the rubber bands that come with them. Wrap string several times around one of the pins in the lower left corner, and then use the placement of the rest of the pins to show how slope is found—rise over run. Up three pins and over two—what does a line with that slope look like? You can also use the middle of the board as the origin to show the result of negative slope.
  o The Geometers' Sketchpad is software that allows students to visualize geometric forms, manipulate them, and solve proofs, all in vivid color! Students can explore equations for lines, curves, and shapes, which helps students develop geometric reasoning skills.

✓ All of the techniques to develop mental-math skills will eventually build mathematics confidence.

o Make sure that students are not so overwhelmed by the timed nature of those activities that they give up entirely. Simply slow the activity down until all are comfortable.

o If a student is far behind the rest of the class in developing math confidence, give her similar problems with simpler numbers. For example, instead of simplifying the fraction $\frac{86}{129}$, have the student simplify the fraction $\frac{18}{36}$. Both fractions reduce to $\frac{2}{3}$.

Differences in Problem-Solving Approaches

Another set of skills that girls believe they have trouble with in mathematics are those involved in solving problems. The question here, as we mentioned before, is whether these skill sets are learned or innate. A recent study indicates that math problem-solving skills in children up through the third grade show no appreciable gender differences (Lachance & Mazzocco, 2006), and it was suggested that this lack of difference may reflect the efforts of educators to improve girls' math performance. The idea that, perhaps, in the lower levels, girls and boys have equal skills and that differences found later may be based on environmental factors was not given as a possible answer for the findings. Recent research indicating that math achievement for girls is connected to gender equity provides some support for the notion that very young girls are as good as boys at math and it is cultural expectations that create the difference (Guiso, Monte, Sapienza, & Zingales, 2008).

Problem solving can be based on facility with concepts. First-grade girls were more likely to use some counting device, such as their fingers, whereas their male age-mates were more likely to use retrieval to solve math problems (Carr & Davis, 2001). The belief is that students with fluent retrieval of math facts are quicker in conceptual development because they use less time with more basic tasks. International studies have found that young girls in other countries have similar math-fact-retrieval ability as boys (Huang, 1993; Lummis & Stevenson, 1990), so one solution for girls in the United States to improve problem-solving ability may be acquiring automaticity with basic math, such as times tables and addition facts.

When students from the United States were compared to students in other countries, the finding for all nations in the study was that, by the end of high school, males do better on tests of mathematics than females (Penner, 2003). An early study discovered that Japanese girls scored better than U.S. boys in the application of concepts to problems, a skill at which U.S. boys consistently score better than U.S. girls. The scores of Japanese boys on those same skills were better than the Japanese girls, so even though Japanese children are better at applying concepts than U.S. children, the relationship between girls and boys remains the same (Lummis & Stevenson, 1990). The suggestion was that, at that time, there was room for improvement in math skills for students from the United States and that a leading problem for American girls is a lack of facility with math facts retrieval. However, remember that in gender equitable countries, girls do better than boys in math (Guiso et al., 2008), so perhaps the best solution is to make sure that girls *believe* they have equal skills.

What all of this means is that girls can improve their skills in mathematics as long as the effort to do so begins early. However, the general consensus is that by the end of high school, the average scores for girls are likely to remain somewhat lower than the average scores for boys. Remember, that average means that there will be girls with superior mathematics abilities who will be at the top of the class. Improving girls' math skills will likely lead to narrowing the gap, with the result that more girls will major in mathematics and related courses in college, increasing the numbers of women in computational careers.

SUGGESTIONS FOR APPLYING THE THEORY TO YOUR CLASSROOM

✓ Problem solving for very young children can begin with all types of puzzles and any other activity where the answer is not known at the beginning. If girls ask for help, encourage your students to work on their own for a while. You may have more success with younger children because they haven't had experience with a great deal of problem solving and, therefore, may not have decided they will have trouble.

  o Simple problems may include having the students decide what the best way to proceed with doing something is. These problems begin with, "How would you go about . . . ?"

  o For young students, problems that are more complex give the opportunity for students to work together. This will enable students to share their strategies so that all students may expand their problem-solving repertoire. Problems may involve exercises from the text or ones that are taken from real life, such as balancing a budget.

  o Questions of any kind can give students practice with problem-solving skills, so encourage the other teachers in your school to have students work independently in their classes as well. Students can use the statistics functions on a calculator to figure out the mean and standard deviation of grades on a history test.

✓ The TV show NUMB3RS uses math to solve problems, and the Web site www.weallusematheveryday.com provides classroom related activities for each episode. One of the regular characters is a young female professor of mathematics who may serve as a role model for your students.

✓ Problem solving is a major issue with all students, but girls in particular tend to look for a solution that they believe will gain approval from the adults around them. Coming up with novel solutions is difficult and girls need practice in this area. Here are some suggestions for various ways to practice problem solving:

○ Logic puzzles—There is a great variety of these and all will help. The advantage is that because they are usually stories, they don't seem like math. You will find sources for these in Chapter 8.

○ 24—This math game comes in a variety of levels and students can work on them alone or in groups of two. There is also a computer version of this game that may increase the chance that girls will work on the computer, especially if they work with a friend.

○ There are many math workbooks involving various math puzzles or problem solving found at various outlets for educational materials. You will find some in your local teacher supply store or look on the Web sites listed in Chapter 8.

✓ Giving girls projects where math is required in daily tasks will help them see that math applies to everything they do. These can be either a reality project or simply questions for homework or class group work.

○ Problems involving money or time are some of the earliest math lessons that are grounded in reality.

○ Frequently, math textbooks have questions asking how much an item is going to cost after a certain percentage is taken off. Bring in the sale pages from your local newspaper and have your students figure out how much they can save by shopping at one store as opposed to another.

○ There are various books and programs for activities involved with investing money in the stock market. Fairly young children can learn to find a certain stock in the reports on the Internet or in the newspaper and note what the stock did yesterday and how that was a change from the day before. More advanced students can have a mock portfolio and "buy" and "sell" stock over a period of time, seeing whether they can improve on the fictitious amount of money they were assigned at the beginning of the exercise. Students are usually more interested in this program if they are encouraged to pick companies who manufacture popular items. This will give them insight into the phenomenon of what happened to stock in the Apple company when the iPod was released.

✓ Ask all students to write the justification for the solution to one problem. If a girl has the chance to tell the teacher why she did a problem in a certain way, she may be more willing to move on to the next problem. This will also give students review on postulates and theorems if they have to state the rule they are following. For example, according to the order of operations, the first step is to simplify the terms inside the parentheses before multiplying by the term outside the parentheses.

(Continued)

(Continued)

✓ Make sure that students do the work on these problems. Explain to parents that the problems you have assigned are skill building and that if they help their daughter she will not learn the skills. Tell the students that they are not to ask for help but to do the best they can. This is *very* hard for girls who have been given a lot of reinforcement and praise for asking questions. Do not have these problems count for a grade until you are sure that all students are comfortable with problem solving. Most students, once they learn the techniques, love these exercises.

People Orientation Preference

From the first day of life, girls are predisposed to look at faces rather than at objects and boys the other way around (Connellan et al., 2000). As children develop, that preference continues, and girls are better able than boys to identify correctly emotional information in others based on facial expressions (McClure, 2000). Whether this preference for using the human face for information is the genesis or not, women prefer occupations that lean toward the people end of a people-things continuum (Lippa, 1998), and math is seen by both men and women as tending more toward the things end of that same scale (Morgan, Isaac, & Sansone, 2001; Webb, Lubinski, & Benbow, 2002).

The question for teachers is whether or not they can present mathematics as a people-oriented subject. Because girls do well in the basic skills of math, if the subject appealed to them, girls would probably be more inclined to continue studying math. Interest in a subject is a major factor in whether or not individuals persist with that subject. So not only do girls need to see that women are involved in careers using mathematics but also they need to be able to find personal involvement and satisfaction in those careers.

SUGGESTIONS FOR APPLYING THE THEORY TO YOUR CLASSROOM

✓ If you overhear your students, either girls or boys, making some reference to the belief that math is a male domain or that girls can't do well in math, make sure that you do something to counteract that belief. Pointing out girls who have done well on a math project will probably not have the effect you want, as both boys and girls may see that as false encouragement.

✓ When you critique student's projects, be sure to focus on what was done and not the manner in which it was done. True, the girls' projects may be tidier, better organized, or follow your directions better than the boys' projects, but attention should be directed to the math. Were the answers correct? Was the question answered? One way to make sure that each student gets similar feedback is to use a rubric.

✓ Invite professionals in computational fields to your class to describe what they do. Students may be surprised to find out that tax preparers are involved with their clients' lives and that bookkeepers don't spend all their time by themselves balancing the books.

✓ If girls are people oriented, then plan for cooperative activities involving several students working together. Begin each unit with a real question that uses the new information as part of the solution.

  o For example, before introducing percentages in elementary school, show students what the percentage mark looks like and then give them pages from the newspaper. Their task will be to find all the percentages on the page and in what context they find those marks.

  o As a review, give worksheets to pairs of students that they will solve together. Have students test each other on basic skills, such as the multiplication tables.

  o Teach students to play bridge. This is a collaborative game that requires excellent math skills, but if you don't focus on the math, students probably won't realize how much math they are using.

Manipulatives

In class, girls who listen well and who want to please adults hear the teacher say not to touch and, perhaps, internalize those requests. We noted earlier that this may be the reason girls are not as likely to manipulate materials in the classroom (Honigsfeld & Dunn, 2003; Jones et al., 2000). Certainly math requires a lot of physical involvement on the part of the student, and I have long believed that one of the problems that girls have with math is that the subject is hard to learn by just reading it or listening to the teacher; you actually have to work problems, and lots of them, to become fluent in math. Girls will do their homework as directed by their teacher, but many will not do much else. Additionally, because of the social constraints against math for girls, they may be reluctant to use math in their daily life, which would give them practice with the concepts.

SUGGESTIONS FOR APPLYING THE THEORY TO YOUR CLASSROOM

✓ Spend a day looking for all of the ways that math is used in your students' lives. From finding out how much it costs to fill the family car with gas to looking for the correct page number for homework questions, students are usually astounded when they realize that they are involved with numbers all the time. When students realize that math is much more than what they do in math class, you may be able to get them to be more willing to involve themselves in math.

(Continued)

(Continued)

✔ We have seen that research indicates that girls will put their hands on materials in the classroom but are more likely to do so when the group is all girls. If you cannot arrange single-sex groups for these activities, then either have students work by themselves or in pairs.

o Tangrams or similar puzzles are colorful and girls enjoy matching shapes.
o Logic puzzles involving placement of colored paperclips or other colored objects by following the rules of the puzzle will appeal to girls.
o Some girls will find Sudoku puzzles interesting.
o SET is a collaborative game that will give girls an advantage because of their superior perceptual-speed skills; they are usually quick to see relationships among various shapes.
o Math workbooks are available where the student solves basic equations and then uses the answers to create pictures or patterns. Some are listed in the materials in Chapter 8.

Exact Solutions

I have asked my female students why they dislike math, and one of the most common complaints is that the answers are so exact; there is no wiggle room. As one girl said, "In an essay, I know that if I keep putting down words, I'll either get the right answer or, at least, give the teacher enough information to believe I know the right answer, but in math, you either get it or you don't." We have seen that girls value mastery of a subject rather than high performance (Kenney-Benson et al., 2006), and that is key to understanding this difficulty in math. Boys simply want to know whether they got the right answer or not, whereas many girls understand that it is possible to get the right answer with an incorrect method. Just putting down the answer doesn't let the girl know if she totally understands how to solve the problem. To make sure that the teacher understands what she did and why, she wants to tell the teacher more than just the answer, and math problems usually don't allow for that.

SUGGESTIONS FOR APPLYING THE THEORY TO YOUR CLASSROOM

✔ Don't grade the final answers; grade the process—did the student use a correct method to solve the problem. My students always found this technique very frustrating, especially when I would put several different ways to solve the problem on the board, but in the end, they realized that only by doing the problem correctly can the right answer be found.

✓ Have students make up their own problems to go with the math being studied in class at the time. This is another attempt to get the students to focus on the process and not on the answer.

✓ Require all students to explain why they selected the method they did to solve a problem. Lacking confidence in their attack skills is a common weak spot for girls. When I have made my students tell me why they used the method they did, they are usually right, but then they go on to say that they are not sure they are right and ask if this other method would work better? They second-guess themselves a great deal.

✓ If a student does not understand what a question on a test is asking, instead of not answering the question, have your students write down what difficulty they encountered in the problem. When you go over the test, the student will then be able to remember what she was thinking at the time. You are likely to find out that the student was on the right track but lacked the confidence to continue. If that is a common occurrence, point out to the student that not answering and giving the wrong answer has the same result, so there is a benefit in trying to answer a question.

WHAT CAN BE DONE TO HELP?

Girls may open their math textbooks with trepidation because of a host of factors that have nothing to do with how well they can learn the subject. We have already covered some of the issues that plague girls and result in perceiving math as not girl friendly. Add to that negative climate a verbal learning approach and it is no wonder that many girls are convinced that they can't do math.

Remember, math used to be for girls, so there must be ways to approach the subject so that girls can succeed. What follows are areas that will help create a classroom environment that will enable girls to achieve in mathematics followed by specific suggestions for those areas.

Early Introduction

The observation is that, in the early years of school, girls and boys are equal in math ability and performance, but girls fall farther and farther behind boys as they progress through school (Beller & Gafni, 1996; Lachance & Mazzocco, 2006; Lloyd et al., 2005). So, whatever you do, do it early. Remember that by third grade girls believed that they were not as good as boys at math, even though their grades were equal (Dickhäuser & Meyer, 2006; Lummis & Stevenson, 1990).

This is particularly true for spatial relations, which probably are part of the skills necessary for geometry. In the past, geometry was not introduced early and, even then, usually as two-dimensional (area) rather than three-dimensional (volume) concepts (Casey et al., 2001). The integrated mathematics curricula popular a few years ago combined algebra and geometry, but only began in middle school and did not address the lack of geometry and spatial tasks in the lower grades. It is hard to determine whether spatial skills are different in very young children or if educational opportunities could ameliorate the differences between girls and boys because most of the research has been done with individuals who are in middle school and above (Casey et al.; Friedman, 1995), and there is little instruction in spatial properties early in school.

One early study involving children from kindergarten to Grade 12 found that there were no differences in spatial ability in very young children and assumed that the relative verbal fluency of the young girls compensated for their deficits in spatial ability (Johnson & Meade, 1987). This same study pointed out the male advantage in spatial skills began about the fourth grade and widened thereafter. The researchers did not comment on the evidence that the girls were doing as well as the boys in the early grades. The point is that there is no definitive answer about when gender differences in spatial skills begin. Additionally, spatial skills are traditionally not part of early math instruction, so there is no way to know if girls could do better if they were given the opportunity.

SUGGESTIONS FOR APPLYING THE THEORY TO YOUR CLASSROOM

✓ If you teach in an elementary school, encourage the teachers in kindergarten and Grades 1 and 2 to provide lessons that involve volume and surface area. Simply having children play with various sized containers will help.

o Base 10 cube sets, which teach volume and the metric system, can be used in many ways. Cuisenaire rods provide excellent examples to help develop an understanding of volume.

o Girls are usually interested in geoboards and other methods to see how the shape of objects can be determined by the edges, such as drawing pictures with string. Students put pins on the edges of a frame and then connect string to one pin winding the string around the pins across the frame creating a design.

o Make sure that all of your students are comfortable with using both English and metric rulers. Use rulers to measure their desks, the length of their feet and hands, or almost anything in the classroom.

○ Give students practice measuring volume and comparing the volumes of similar containers. Sets of measuring cups can be used to determine volume of water (if you are comfortable with the mess that will result), sand, or bits of cereal.

○ Weigh balloons before and after blowing them up. Children are frequently fascinated to discover that air has mass and that the fuller the balloon, the more it weighs.

○ Every time something needs to be counted in the classroom—students, chairs, papers to hand out, and the like—make that counting purposeful. Assign one student each day to collect all the numbers that the class uses (other than in a math lesson) in a school day. For example, "We counted how many students were present at the beginning of school, we drew numbers to decide who used the computers first, and we read the temperature for the day."

✓ One second-grade teacher had her students find out the length of an average blue whale and mark it on the wall in front of the classroom. They used blue painter's tape, which comes off painted surfaces easily and can be written on with markers, to indicate where the flukes started, where the blowhole should be, and other important parts of the whale. For comparison, you could also have the students compare the length of a school bus to the whale or, perhaps, the height of their teacher compared to the length of the whale. Although this was part of a science lesson, math skills were involved in the measuring and spatial skills were used in understanding the size of the animal.

Attitude Change

Remember, at least part of the problem is that girls do not believe that they can be successful in math. We have seen that very young girls do not share that attitude with older students, so the issue is to be proactive early to make sure that girls do not develop a negative attitude toward math.

Families

Whether or not girls see themselves as competent in math is directly correlated with the beliefs of their families about their future in math (Räty & Kasanen, 2007; Tenenbaum & Leaper, 2003). Mothers were more likely to buy toys that were science or math related for their sons, but both parents were more likely to be involved with their daughters in science and math related activities. The explanation for this was that the parents perceived that the daughters required more assistance in this area (Jacobs & Bleeker, 2004). However, for both sons and daughters, future involvement in math and science was directly related to the promotion of those subjects by their parents.

SUGGESTIONS FOR APPLYING THE THEORY TO YOUR CLASSROOM

✓ Do everything you can to point out to the families of your students how well the girls are doing in math. Every now and then, assign an exercise for homework that requires the students to demonstrate a math fact to someone at home.

✓ Be careful about posting student work in the classroom. Unless all students have work posted, those who do not may see that as an indication that they are not doing well. Tessellation worksheets and figures drawn on the Geometer's Sketchpad will give everyone a chance to shine.

✓ Invite family members to the class to describe how they use numbers or math in their jobs.

Teachers

Even though education has made a substantial effort to reverse the idea that girls can't do math, that conviction is still prevalent. If the teacher believes that math is a male domain, that will certainly reflect the way she or he reacts to student progress (Ding, Song, & Richardson, 2006; Keller, 2001). Girls were more likely to ascribe their lack of success in math to a lack of assistance from teachers (Lloyd et al., 2005). If the teachers are working under the misapprehension that girls will find math more difficult, then teachers may be reluctant to offer help when they don't believe it will result in success.

SUGGESTIONS FOR APPLYING THE THEORY TO YOUR CLASSROOM

✓ A community college math department has a day each year where local schoolteachers are invited to the college to hear speakers on math and to see and practice new approaches to math education. This event also provides a place for teachers to network and share methods that they find useful in their own classrooms. You could ask your local college math department either to do something like this or to come to your school to talk to teachers.

✓ Invite teachers from other departments or grades to your classroom so that they can see how well girls do in math and how interested they are.

✓ Prepare a class skit that involves math to present to the whole school. Students could be triangles and circles and talk about their properties and where they are found in the world, for example.

Students

If the families and the teachers are still sending the message that math is hard for girls, it is quite understandable that some girls find math hard. However, as we have already seen that attitude is changing. In Australia, a recent study found that girls and boys reported that girls in middle school were likely to do better in math than boys (Forgasz et al., 2004). Girls attending schools in Canada got better grades than boys on a basic assessment of arithmetic skills and knew that effort was directly related to performance. However, even though the girls performed better than the boys on a standardized test, the girls were still not as confident that they would do as well as the boys (Lloyd et al., 2005).

Clearer Instruction

So what can the teacher do to improve the chances that girls will do well in math? Remember that girls use words to frame their memory and start from there. When I teach math, I say out loud every step I'm doing and the reason for it. My students tell me that this method helps them develop the narrative that they need to solve problems on their own.

Girls rely heavily on traditional methods to solve problems, especially when those methods are directly taught in the classroom (Gallagher & De Lisi, 1994). This starts early, and young girls who are in the third grade or earlier solve problems the way they have been instructed, whereas boys are more likely to come up with more abstract and novel strategies that indicate conceptual understanding (Fennema, Carpenter, Jacobs, Franke, & Levi, 1998). If you rely too heavily on making students follow every step, girls may have trouble coming up with different approaches. Model flexible approaches, but tell the students what you are doing and why you are going in another direction. Girls need that even though they may complain that they need to know exactly what you want them to do.

SUGGESTIONS FOR APPLYING THE THEORY TO YOUR CLASSROOM

✓ When you are teaching anything in math, make sure that you say *out loud* every step you are doing and the rationale for that step. When I tutor girls who are having trouble with math, the single most effective strategy I use is simply to tell the student everything I am doing. You will find an example titled Verbalizing Math in Chapter 8.

(Continued)

(Continued)

✓ When a student asks you how to solve a problem or if they have chosen the correct method to solve a problem, do not answer the question directly. Ask them what they know about the problem, what other problems they have solved that were similar, or why they chose the method that they did. If the student tells you that she has no idea how to begin to solve the problem, start by doing a short review: What have we just been studying? What kind of problems do you remember that we have done recently? Do you see similar words or symbols in this problem?

Focus on Process, Not Product

Everyone who has taught girls has had to deal with the student who insists on knowing if she got the *right* answer. This can be a problem when you are trying to focus on the process involved in solving problems instead of the product. This may seem strange because, in general, girls are concerned with working hard, understanding the process, and doing what the teacher asks. They judge their success by teacher feedback (Kenney-Benson et al., 2006). Success is determined by whether or not they have the correct response to a problem, but their focus is on the process and not the product. If they get the wrong answer, girls can become distressed and are more likely than boys to internalize that distress (Pomerantz et al., 2002). The problem is that the girl sees the larger difficulty—not that she got the wrong answer to this problem, but that this wrong answer demonstrates that she doesn't understand how to do this type of problem and she is going to have trouble with *all* of these problems in the future. Every time a girl gets a wrong answer, it adds to the evidence, in her mind, of her math inability.

What I frequently do when working with students, both boys and girls, who are having trouble is to simplify the examples.

SUGGESTIONS FOR APPLYING THE THEORY TO YOUR CLASSROOM

✓ Older versions of texts frequently have simpler examples.

✓ Use the same problem format, but use small numbers. Students can more easily intuit the answer and then work backward to figure out what they did. For example, a problem asks for the length of each side of a box if the perimeter is 35 inches and one side is 7.5 inches. If the student has trouble deciding how to begin solving this problem, give the student a simpler version: What is the length of each side if the perimeter is 6 inches and one side is 2 inches? The student can draw this problem or build it with Cuisenaire rods and figure out what operations will get the solution. Then that solution can be used as a model to solve the more complicated problem.

✓ If your students have trouble with word problems, teach them the method that my math teacher taught me years ago, called "Box the Operator." You will find this method illustrated in Chapter 8.

✓ When you have a chance, solve the same problem several different ways. You will get a chorus of, "But what is the right way to solve the problem?" from the girls. Point out that each method works and that they may find that one method works better for them than another.

   ○ Challenge students to find different ways to solve problems.
   ○ Make sure that, even at the youngest levels, students are encouraged to explore alternative routes. If you find it hard to think of other approaches, ask another teacher for help. What you will find is that each of you will have a slightly different way of solving the same problem and that you can offer her class your perspective on problem solving and vice versa.

Peer Influence

There is no question that all adolescents and preadolescents are influenced by the opinions and behaviors of their peer group. Girls tend to focus on one other person or on an individual within a group (Benenson & Heath, 2006). Consequently, the loss of a friend upsets a girl more than it does a boy (Benenson & Christakos, 2003), as the loss represents a greater proportion of her friends. If the price of friendship is conforming to the opinions of their peers, girls will do just that.

I have taught girls who really liked math. It was obvious, not because they told me, but because of the way they behaved in class and the attention they paid to their work. In my pre-algebra class, Sue was a classic example. She liked doing math puzzles, she would solve extra problems just for fun, and she was fascinated by the application of math to everyday situations. At the beginning of the next year, she entered my algebra class saying that she was so glad to be back in math class. During the year, a girl with whom she was friendly began to become influential in the class. One day, after having been unable to solve a particularly tricky word problem, the powerful peer announced to the class that math was unnecessary and she couldn't wait to be finished with it. Then she turned to Sue who was sitting beside her and asked Sue to agree with her. Sue looked briefly at me and then agreed that math was not fun. For the rest of the year, Sue did adequate work, but the spark she had in math was gone. I asked her to come and chat, but she always found some excuse. I left after that year, so I have no knowledge about whether or not Sue ever did reconnect with math—I would bet she did not unless she made friends with another peer who liked math. I wish I had known then what I know now and I would have tried harder to get Sue back as well as convince the peer that she was better in math than she believed.

SUGGESTIONS FOR APPLYING THE THEORY TO YOUR CLASSROOM

✓ If you notice that a group of girls has decided that math is not for them or that math is too hard, divide them up the next time you put students in groups. One way to make your tactic less obvious is to introduce probability and randomness to the class as a way to make group assignment more fair. Find some method to sort students into groups, which could be dice, names drawn out of a hat (a sorting hat?), or assigning numbers using the calculator as a random number generator—whatever is appropriate at your students' level. The students can keep track of the members of each group and find out after a period of time if the method is truly random.

✓ All of the activities to see how math is all around us will provide examples of how students can't escape math. Point out to the reluctant students that a minimum level of math proficiency is needed in everyone's life.

MATH AND GIRLS

Many girls have the impression that math is not for them or are somewhat unimpressed with their ability to do math. Helping girls see that they can do math in a way that better suits their learning strengths will provide models for them to learn a variety of subjects, not just math. They will also find that facility with math is useful in a variety of areas that may not seem to be involved at all, such as solving problems with everyday life.

ANSWERS TO QUIZ

1. B—Boys scored better on math tests, but only by two points at all three levels, Grades 4, 6, and 12 (in 2005). On the other hand, on 2005 reading scores, fourth-grade girls scored six points higher than boys, eighth-grade girls scored 10 points higher, and 12th-grade girls scored 13 points higher than boys (National Center for Educational Statistics [NCES], 2007b).

2. C—Girls and boys in eighth grade were equal in meeting or exceeding proficiency in math skills. Girls and boys were about equal for beginning skills (98.8% of girls and 98.3% of boys), and girls were slightly better in numerical operations and beginning problem solving (84.1% of girls and 82.8% of boys). However, for moderately complex procedures and reasoning, more boys obtained proficiency (32.6% of boys and 25.6 % of girls) (Snyder et al., 2006).

3. C—Girls and boys were equally proficient in numerical operations and beginning problem solving in 12th grade (96.8% of girls and 96.6% of boys), but boys were more proficient in moderately complex procedures and reasoning (60.6% of boys and 56.7% of girls) and multistep problem solving and algebra (8.8% of boys and 5.1% of girls) (Snyder et al., 2006).

4. B—Boys scored better on the math portion of the 2007 SAT, by 34 points. Boys only averaged two points higher in critical reading, but girls averaged 11 points higher on the writing portion (College Board, 2006).

5. A—Girls earned more high school credits in math and science by graduation. In 2005, girls earned on average 7.3 science and math credits and boys earned 7.1 by the end of high school (Shettle et al., 2007).

6. A—Girls had higher GPAs in math and science. In 2005, the average GPA for female high school graduates in math and science courses was 2.76 and for male graduates it was 2.56 (Shettle et al., 2007).

7. C—Girls and boys were about even for credits received in advanced math. Comparing high school graduates from 2000 who took math, 70.5% of the girls had a credit in Algebra II, whereas only 64.5% of the boys had that credit and girls still have the advantage in pre-calculus, 27.9% to 25.4%. For higher math courses, more boys obtain credits, but not by a lot. Of male graduates 12% got a credit in calculus compared to 11.1% of female graduates, and AP calculus was similar, 8.5% males compared to 7.3% females (Snyder et al., 2006).

8. B—Boys received more bachelor degrees in mathematics this year. However, girls received 46% of the bachelor degrees in math, and that figure has dropped a little over the past ten years. In 1995, 47% of bachelor degrees in math were awarded to girls (Snyder et al., 2006).

9. C—Girls received more bachelor degrees in SME areas in 2004, primarily because of the large number of degrees received in psychology (77.8%) and the biological sciences (62.5%) (National Science Foundation, 2007).

10. A—Girls received the fewest engineering degrees. Engineering was the SME area that had the fewest females obtaining bachelor degrees, with only 20.5% of the degrees going to girls. But that was up from 17.3% in 1994 (National Science Foundation, 2007).

5

Teaching Science to the Female Brain

Although some of my students appeared to be afraid of math, few of the girls had the same strong reaction to science. Many of my students really enjoyed biology, and some liked physics as well, but more were simply indifferent to science (Gould, Weeks, & Evans, 2003). It has always seemed to me that the problem is not that girls don't like science but that they don't *think* that they will like science (Jenkins & Nelson, 2005). One of my students told me, about six weeks into a physical science course, that she was surprised that she actually liked the class. She said that she thought science was for nerds and she didn't consider herself a nerd. For girls, especially in middle and high school, much of what interests them is colored by what they perceive to be acceptable by others, and for some, being a nerd is not popular in their social groups. Even after years of emphasis on math and science in coed schools, girls are staying away from technology and computers, and the problem is how to get girls interested.

We know from the chapter on mathematics that girls get better grades in high school in science and math courses than boys do, but do they take as many science courses? Is there a difference in the way girls perform in science? How well *do* they do? See how many of the following questions you can answer correctly.

QUIZ

Respond to the following statements by indicating whether the statement best describes (a) girls/women, (b) boys/men, or (c) both girls and boys/both men and women

1. Enrolled in more biology and advanced-placement (AP) biology courses in 2005

2. Enrolled in more chemistry and AP chemistry courses in 2005

3. Enrolled in more physics and AP physics courses in 2005

4. Enrolled in more of all three of the major sciences, biology, chemistry, and physics, in 2005

5. Were more likely to take physics in 2006, out of college-bound students taking the SAT

6. Received more bachelor degrees in biological sciences in 2004

7. Received fewer bachelor degrees in computer science from 1995 to 2004

8. Are more likely to use a computer as part of their job

9. Are more often employed in the computer and mathematics occupations

10. Were more employed as veterinarians in 2004

Answers are on page 113.

Once you check the answers to these questions, you will see that women are more involved in the various areas of science than may be commonly believed, and with few exceptions, that number is growing. Engineering is still a field where women are vastly underrepresented. In 2005, only 13.8% of individuals practicing in the architectural and engineering professions were women (U.S. Bureau of Labor Statistics, 2006). However, more women than men take courses in the biological sciences, and as those numbers grow, more women will be employed in professions requiring scientific knowledge. For example, although the majority of veterinarians practicing in 2004 were men, this will change as the new female graduates fill the profession.

WHY GIRLS DON'T LIKE SCIENCE

When girls take science courses, they frequently do well in them, but the fact is that many girls don't pursue science as a career (American Association of University Women [AAUW], 2008). Recall the list of women mentioned in the quiz in the introduction. They are just a few of a long list of prominent female scientists, so the evidence is there that women can be successful in science, but lately more and more girls are staying away from technical careers (Sax, 2008). So what is the problem?

Access (or the Lack of It)

Complaints made by women about science include the belief that their participation is not encouraged, creating impediments to their entrance into the professions associated with particular sciences (Blickenstaff, 2005; Hodgson, 2000). I watched as a promising young scientist was excluded from a departmental meeting, and when she complained, she was told that they must have forgotten to tell her about the meeting. The problem was that the rest of the members of the department were all older men and she was young, female, and very capable. One member of the department who supported her revealed that the rest of the old guard found her quick mind and new ideas somewhat intimidating. If I thought that this story was a rare event, I wouldn't have included it, but over and over, I have heard similar stories where women either were directly denied access to full participation in the sciences or were encouraged to take a subordinate role.

Part of the pressure for women to avoid the sciences comes from society in general. Although the attitude about women in the biological and health sciences is positive and reflects the influx of women into those areas, society continues to consider engineering and the physical sciences traditionally masculine domains (Kennedy & Parks, 2000; Steele, James, & Barnett, 2002). In fact, the perception is that girls who like science are less feminine, even though when asked, girls who like science viewed themselves as slightly more feminine than other girls (Breakwell et al., 2003). As more women enter the science professions, which is bound to happen because, ever so slowly, more women are receiving degrees in these areas, the pressure to admit women to full participation will increase. This will make a difference eventually, but progress has been slow in some areas.

Part of the problem of access is that if women choose to have a family, the time that they take away from the pursuit of their interests is held against them. The result is that they lose their place in line, so to speak, and are less likely to be promoted at the same rate as their male colleagues. They will earn less money, which may be the result of choosing to work part time or choosing to work in lower-level positions where the schedule is more regular but where the opportunity for remuneration is less than high-status jobs (Sasser, 2005). Working in areas that are more family friendly, such as primary or secondary education and nonprofit companies, provides better chances for a good family life, but these pursuits tradition-ally pay less than the more competitive positions in research or tertiary education. As a result, some women who major in science decide to pursue careers in related fields. Their scientific training is an advantage in business or commercial production, where they will receive adequate compensation for their skills as well as time to raise a family (Miller, Blessing, & Schwartz, 2006). A mathematician who worked for NASA for more than 30 years agreed that women with science and technical backgrounds are finding business to be a family friendly place where they can succeed, but she feels that this is a fairly recent trend, as she did not find it to be true years ago.

One phenomenon that has occurred as women enter the sciences is dis-couraging. That observation is that as women increase in numbers in any field, the status of that field drops and men begin to move out of it (Hodgson, 2000). The opposite has been seen in a female field that has seen an increase in male participation—nursing. As more men become nurses, the status of nurses is increasing and, not surprisingly, the salaries are rising as well, particularly for the men (Kalist, 2002).

SUGGESTIONS FOR APPLYING THE THEORY TO YOUR CLASSROOM

✓ Invite women who are in business or industry who have a science background to talk about how they made their career decisions. Encourage them to discuss the results of their decision and whether they would make the same decision now.

✓ If you are close to a university, find out if there are female students who will be willing to come talk to your students. These young women are closer to the age of your students, and what they say may resonate with your students.

✓ Do not avoid talking about the problems that women can have in breaking into the "hard" sciences and encourage the female scientists who visit your class to talk about their experiences moving up the career ladder. Some women will report that they have had great difficulty and others will have positive stories to tell. Most will have advice for your students to help them anticipate some difficulties.

✓ When you invite scientists to your classroom, make sure to ask them to include stories about how they work their family lives into their jobs. If any student in your school has a female family member who is a practicing scientist, make sure to invite her to speak to your class. The national associations of women scientists, engineers, and mathematicians all have information about how to balance a career and a family.

Science Is Uninteresting

Remember that from the day of their birth, girls are more interested in looking at faces and boys are more interested in looking at objects (Connellan et al., 2000). This is considered part of the reason girls are more interested in people and less in things. The sciences that girls are interested in, such as biology, are seen as people oriented or, at the very least, are seen as necessary steps on the path to a people-oriented health-related profession, such as medicine (Miller et al., 2006).

When I was in middle school, the only person who supported me in my interest in science was my female science teacher. At some point, my classmates made remarks about my absorption in the subject we were studying—my memory is that we were dissecting frogs—something to the effect that my interest wasn't very feminine. My science teacher, who was my ideal of feminine beauty and the only person in the school taller than I was, pointed out the accomplishments of the Curies and other women scientists, which made me feel better. My classmates in the girls' high school I attended later were as baffled by my interest in science as I was by their lack of interest. I now know that my middle school science teacher made all the difference and what helped me was the knowledge that there were other women in science. It doesn't take much to help a girl believe she can be a scientist and that help may come from just one person.

Elementary school girls and boys like science equally, and both groups expected to have more difficulty with science compared to other subjects (Andre et al., 1999). However, parents of those elementary school students expected boys to do better in science, partially because jobs related to science were seen as part of the male domain. Both girls and boys report that they find science less likely to afford them the chance to pursue interpersonal goals and more likely to offer extrinsic rewards. The difference is that girls are usually uninterested in careers that do not afford them the opportunities to connect with others, whereas that does not seem to matter to boys who are very interested in pursuing careers that they perceive will offer extrinsic rewards (Lubinski, Webb, Morelock, & Benbow, 2001; Morgan et al., 2001).

At least part of the problem is that girls may not even consider majoring in science, technology, engineering, and math (STEM) courses because of their perception of the lifestyle associated with people in those areas (Kahle, 1989). The implication is that scientists are nerds who only socialize with others with similar interests. The science oriented television shows such as *Mythbusters* and *CSI* have provided some female characters who serve as models to show students that scientists are not necessarily isolated in a laboratory but work with a wide variety of people. This is a mixed blessing because however involved the women are in these shows, in each case, the head of the lab is a man.

Collaborative Learning Style

Girls prefer to learn as part of a group, and the observation has been made that in same-sex groups in a coed science classroom, girls engage in collaborative and cooperative activities combined with lots of conversation about the activity (Guzzetti, 2001). In a male-dominated classroom, which is likely to be the case especially in physics and engineering, the atmosphere is apt to be competitive and the focus will be on individual success (Zohar & Sela, 2003). Girls want to see how everything is connected, and their way of achieving that is to discuss how each member in the group perceives the topic. Even if you try to get most girls to work by themselves, they will prefer to collaborate with another student.

It is possible that the science teacher may perceive a girl's need to examine a problem in the totality by discussing approaches with the teacher or with other students as an indication that the student does not understand or cannot solve the problem on her own. One young woman who asked her physics teacher for help with a problem set was encouraged to drop the class because the teacher viewed her questioning as lack of understanding when it was simply her need to collaborate on a solution (Sax, 2005).

When I took chemistry in high school, my teacher and I crossed swords over this need to collaborate. I was perfectly happy working by myself, but the girl at the lab station next to me was unsure about what we were supposed to be doing in lab and would constantly ask me questions. When I answered, the teacher viewed that as "talking in class," so many of my lab reports were marked down for talking. What I wasn't aware of then was that my fellow student needed a collaborative learning experience to understand the material. I didn't need that approach, but I did realize that I learned the material better when I was able to talk it over with another person. This experience pointed out to me that, perhaps, I had a future as a science teacher and I tried to remember that experience in my own science classes by encouraging the students to talk over what they were doing with one another.

SUGGESTIONS FOR APPLYING THE THEORY TO YOUR CLASSROOM

✓ Traditionally, laboratory work is performed in groups, usually two students working together. That is perfect for girls, and if you can arrange it, especially for girls who may find science a bit daunting, make sure that the groups are single-sex.

✓ In physics and chemistry, where solving problems can be a large part of the curriculum, suggest that girls form problem study groups where they can work together. If your schedule permits, you can give the students time during the school day to do this, or they can get together after school or at home to work in these groups.

✓ Once a lab exercise is completed, have each lab group come to the front of the room to present the data that resulted from the exercise. This gives students a chance to hear various solution paths as well as get a feel for the variety of answers that can result from the same lab experience. Second graders can do this just as well as older students. This allows students to connect with others to make the whole class a collaborative group.

✓ Although girls like to work with others, they generally work with the same partner. The problem is that the girls in that pair tend to get in the habit of solving problems in the same way. Mixing up groups allows students to work with a variety of approaches. Yes, some girls will resist this because they are comfortable working with friends. Make it part of the lab procedure that lab partners have to be switched each week, chapter, or unit.

✓ You want girls to develop confidence in participating in science. In coed classrooms, boys are more likely to take charge of class discussions, so single-sex groups, even in a coed classroom, will give girls a chance to develop confidence in their science ability (Cox & Fisher, 2008).

Science Background

We have already covered the fact that parents gave their sons more science related toys than their daughters (Tenenbaum & Leaper, 2003) and that parents were more likely to give scientific explanations for events to sons than daughters (Crowley, Callanan, Tenenbaum, & Allen, 2001). From the beginning, parents may be shaping their children's interests in science unconsciously, but that isn't always true. I was far more fascinated by my brother's Erector set and by the copper-wire antenna he built for our old-fashioned radio than I was by the dolls I was given. Had I been an only child, my exposure to science would have been to help my father garden and to watch my mother, who was an English teacher, put a new plug on the electrical cord of a lamp—an event born of desperation that worked moderately well. At least we never had any fires because of her repairs, although later, when I learned how wiring should work, I never used any of those lamps until I supplied new plugs myself. My family was perplexed by my interests, but they supported me in my pursuit of a career in science. In retrospect, I realize that the key was that they never gave me the impression that science wasn't for girls and they supported me in all of my interests.

Lack of early exposure to science is certainly going to make a difference if only by limiting the way that a child views the world. Explanations for experiences are going to be different for children who have been exposed to lots of scientific knowledge and those who have not. In fourth grade, my son's class was studying plants and the teacher had brought in several different common plants complete with their root systems. The children were to draw the plants, what appeared above and below ground, and label the parts and types of root systems. I was in the classroom on an unrelated matter, when a child asked the teacher what were the funny bumps on the roots of a plant. The teacher didn't know, and my son brought the plant to me. I told him to look at the top of the plant and identify it first. He correctly identified the plant as clover and then, with a look of excitement said, "Oh, the bumps are nitrogen nodules!"

The teacher was astounded, and I explained that he had recently been with his father, a landscape architect, on a job site, and his father had pointed out the clover that had been planted to enrich the soil. His father explained how clover fixes nitrogen in nodules or bumps on the roots. Our son combined that information with his recognition of the top of the plant to get the correct explanation, partially because he had been exposed to that sort of thinking. We took him to lots of science museums, not only because I am a science teacher but also because my husband has a lively interest in science. When our son was young, both of us tried to give him a scientific explanation or observation about events in his life, so he thinks that way today. We didn't have a daughter, but I would like to believe that if we had, we would have given her the same experiences and explanations that we gave our son. Certainly, when I taught in girls' schools, I gave scientific explanations to the students even when the subject had nothing to do with class. I noticed at the time that the girls were very interested in my technical explanations.

Teachers are more likely to call on boys in a coed classroom and explain to them how to do the lab exercise, whereas teachers are more likely to show girls how to do the exercise (Cox & Fisher, 2008). That attitude will demonstrate to girls that the teacher believes that they are not very capable in science or that they need more help than the boys do. The problem is that the girls will ask you what they are to do. Don't answer them directly. Ask them what they think is the first step. An experienced science teacher says to keep your hands in your pockets—make them show you.

It would make sense that children who have a background in science should do better, but that only seems to make a difference in their *interest* in science. A study discovered that it was not a lack of prior knowledge but actually the way the girls believed they would perform that was responsible for girls not doing as well as boys in a physics class (Dresel, Ziegler, Broome, & Heller, 1998). Of course, without prior exposure, girls may believe that they will not do well in physics, not because of lack of experience or knowledge but because they hear from others that girls don't do well in physics. This is especially true for girls with low ability in science (Meece & Jones, 1996). So early exposure to science will help, but only if girls do not get the impression that they will not do well in science or that science is for boys.

SUGGESTIONS FOR APPLYING THE THEORY TO YOUR CLASSROOM

✓ Provide a wide variety of scientific materials for very young students and encourage all students to explore what is available. If you are not sure how to do this easily and inexpensively, go to a local children's science museum or visit the Web site of children's museums or discovery museums for ideas.

  o My son's teacher dug up plants, such as clover and dandelions, roots and all, and washed the dirt off. The children were fascinated by what was below the surface, as well as what was above.

  o Children are usually interested in how to make simple vegetable dyes from plants. One of the most interesting facets of this is why fabric dyed with extracts of beets, red cabbage, coffee, tea, blueberries, onion skins (the brown part), and carrots fade. Because the colors are water soluble, washing causes the color to disappear gradually. It is a simple process to make permanent colors by adding a mordant, which is a chemical means to make a dye resistant to fading. A simple mordant can be made from common kitchen chemicals, and you can find the directions on the Internet.

  o Another facet of the vegetable dying experiment is to use various fabrics and see how well some absorb dye and some do not. Slightly older children may be interested in making dyes and dipping squares of various fabrics in the dye. You need to know what the fabric is made of, so get the fabric from a supplier, but most fabric stores will give you small samples of fabric or at least not charge you much if you tell them what you want the fabric for. Use white or natural colored squares of muslin (cotton), wool, silk, linen, acrylics, nylon, polyester, and blends of all of those fabrics.

  o A third facet of the dying experiment would be to see what accelerates fading. Dye squares of fabric that seem to hold the color the best, dry the squares, and then subject the fabrics to diluted solutions of bleach, color-safe bleach, vinegar, detergent, and lemon juice. Dip some squares in a solution of salt and water, rinse them out, let them dry, and then put them in the bleaching solutions. Finally, leave a dyed square and a salt-treated dyed square in the sun for a week. Keep a dyed sample in a light-tight container for comparison.

✓ Simply getting your students to look carefully at the world around them will start developing the skills necessary for science. Outside your school, mark one-meter squares in the grass with string and large paper clips. If you straighten the outside loop of the clip and stick that in the ground, the smaller loop will hold the string. Give pairs of students magnifying glasses and have them look carefully at what they see in their area. They should draw pictures of plants, animals, or anything else they find in their plot, including trash.

(Continued)

(Continued)

  ✓ If the season, the weather, or the school grounds make it difficult to observe out-side, give students masking tape and have them stick the tape to any surface, such as clothing, rugs, desks, vinyl floors, and the like to see what they can pick up. Actually, any surface other than paper will do as long as the students don't let the tape sit on the surface for long. It will be easier to retrieve the tape if the students fold over one end to make a handle. Then the students should look at what they have picked up with the tape. They may be surprised at what is there that they did not see originally.

  ✓ If science is not your favorite topic and you teach in a self-contained classroom, perhaps you can coteach or swap classes with another teacher who is more comfortable with science, and you can swap by giving instruction in the mate-rial with which you are comfortable.

  ✓ There are many books that describe kitchen-sink science experiments—activities that can be accomplished with common household items and that require easily available equipment. You will find a list of such sources in Chapter 8.

  ✓ Before you take over for a student in a lab exercise, try to talk the child through it. Girls may frequently ask you how to do something when what they are ask-ing is for you to approve of how they are going to do it. Listen carefully when students ask you for information in a lab and answer with another question. "What are we to do next?" should be answered with, "What is the next step that you think is appropriate?" Don't answer before you ask.

Spatial Relationships

Just to remind you, there are three different forms of spatial relation-ships (see Chapter 1 for a full description). You will also remember that girls and boys perform similarly on tasks of spatial visualization; boys have a slight edge in spatial perception; and boys have a bigger advantage in tasks of mental perception (Linn & Petersen, 1985). Given that science studies the world and how manipulations of parts of the world affect events, it would seem that spatial skills would be an advantage in science.

The advent of computer-assisted imaging techniques, such as func-tional magnetic resonance imaging (fMRI), has allowed us to look at the brain as the individual performs various tasks. Research using this tech-nique has uncovered that women use the left side of the brain and part of the right when performing a verbal task, whereas men, doing the same task, appear to use only the left portion of their brain (Shaywitz et al., 1995). Similar studies about the brains of men and women per-forming a spatial task found that men used the right side of their brain and some of the left, whereas women only used the right portion of their brain (Gur et al., 2000).

Of course, this does not guarantee that one sex is better at a task than the other is, but that they use their brains differently for the same task. There seems to be general agreement as to the verbal advantage enjoyed by girls, but even that advantage seems to shrink as people age because of the similarity of verbal intelligence in men and women (Halpern, 2000). However, in discussing cognitive gender differences in spatial tasks, some research states that the differences are too small to make a difference (Hyde, 2005; Spelke, 2005), and other research is sure that boys are much better than girls (Halpern et al., 2007).

Why are we concerned that girls may believe that they do not have good spatial skills? In the past, girls were made to feel that they were not likely to do well in math and science, and consequently, many girls who could have succeeded in these areas did not try (Corbett, Hill, & St. Rose, 2008). That does not mean that all girls could succeed in the STEM areas if they just put their minds to it, and although we are seeing more girls entering the math and technical fields, the numbers are not large. The concern is that if some girls have trouble with spatial relations it may result in discouraging more girls from subjects that require those skills.

Are spatial skills essential to success in science? This well-known example will illustrate this point. Figure 5.1, Piagetian Water-Level Test, presents a drawing of a glass half filled with water, such as that on the left. The subject is then given a picture of a glass without water on about a 45° angle and asked to draw where the level of the water would be in this glass. Traditionally, men are more successful in drawing the correct horizontal line, and many women tend to draw the line as it was in the original drawing.

Figure 5.1   Piagetian Water-Level Test

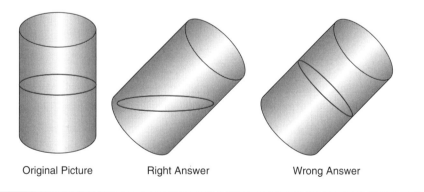

Original Picture   Right Answer   Wrong Answer

What is fascinating is that some female college students who were majoring in physics did not perform as well on this and other similar visual tasks as their male colleagues, so training in the sciences was not enough to overcome this spatial problem (Robert & Harel, 1996).

The question is whether these spatial skills are important to success in science. For a set of skills that are the subject of a great many studies, you would think this would be an important question which needs to be answered. Most of the studies determine whether there are gender differences among the skills, but little information ties these skills directly to science. Even for the water-level test, some successful female physics majors could not provide a correct answer to a situation that involves physical properties of substances. It is quite possible that girls whose spatial skills are not strong might use that as part of a reason not to pursue the sciences in school, but evidence indicates that girls whose spatial skills are not strong can do very well in science.

SUGGESTIONS FOR APPLYING THE THEORY TO YOUR CLASSROOM

✓ There are many ways to help girls improve spatial skills. What follows is a brief list of suggested activities, and you can find others in Chapter 4.

- o Play puzzles—everything from jigsaw to Scrabble, which is, after all, a word puzzle.
- o Play chess, Chinese checkers, Mastermind, or similar games.
- o Make pottery—shaping objects out of clay requires good spatial skills, and firing techniques and the application of glazes are good chemistry lessons.
- o Weave either fabric or baskets.
- o Make mosaics out of small tiles.
- o Make and read maps.
- o Try orienteering—there are various levels for students of different ages and many science museums and scouting programs will offer various versions.
- o Play the card game AC/DC, which will help younger students understand the basics of electrical circuitry.
- o Build pop-up mothers' day cards or other holiday cards. Bring in a few examples so that the students can see how these are made.
- o Build marble roller coasters out of Popsicle sticks glued to science display boards. Depending on the age of your students, the devices can be simple slides or may involve turns, drops, and jumps.
- o Play Noodlers, a game in which students are given cards with pictures on them and various numbers of sticks to separate each picture into its own space; it provides good spatial challenges.

✓ Provide three-dimensional models for various biological subjects, structures of elements and compounds, and our solar system or require that the students make such models.

- o When teaching about atoms, ask your class to figure out what atom they could make using the people in the class. Have all students stand up and become a proton, a neutron, or an electron. Then have them stand so that they approximate the shape of that atom, including forming the different electron shells. Ask them to make the two largest atoms that could be made with the same number of particles as the number of people in the class. Remove one student from the configuration and ask them what effect that has on the atom depending on whether the individual represented a proton, a neutron, or an electron.

✓ Make sure that all data collected is displayed in a table or on a graph. You may have to provide some sort of structure to begin with and then help students learn to display data on their own tables or graphs. For older students, require that they use computer software to produce the graphic displays.

Other Sensory Differences

I cannot find any evidence for this, but some of the problems that girls have with science may be because of the way that young children are exposed to science. In the attempt to interest students in science, many demonstrations in science museums and elsewhere can be loud and unexpected. In the process of an experiment on electrolysis of water, one of my students asked if she could leave the classroom when we put a flame to the gases collected. She said that she had seen the lab done before and the noise from the exploding hydrogen and the flames from putting a glowing stick in the oxygen bothered her. I pointed out that we only had very small amounts of the gases and the hydrogen would only make a pop and the flame would be small. She looked dubious, but was willing to observe from across the room.

We have already discussed that girls' hearing is more sensitive than boys', and the sensitivity to other senses may create problems. Some of the students in my biology classes were genuinely upset at the smells of the preserved specimens that we were to dissect, so I provided paper masks and disposable gloves for them. The virtual frog dissection software is good and may give some girls an acceptable way to discover what the organs look like. Students who use the software will not have an understanding of the dimensionality or the composition of the inside of an animal, but they will learn some of the material. In chemistry, anytime we used sulfur, I had one student who would get nauseated and need to be excused. You may need to make accommodations for these students, but do not allow them to be exempt from the material.

SUGGESTIONS FOR APPLYING THE THEORY TO YOUR CLASSROOM

✓ Older students are less bothered by noise, but if you teach in the lower grades, make sure that girls are aware that a demonstration will result in a loud noise and allow them to view from some distance or give them soft earplugs.

✓ I found that older students were more bothered by smells, and I would bring a large box fan into my lab when we were doing something smelly. Put the fan in the window pointing out to draw the smells away. Some labs have fans for this purpose. If the fan is likely to make the exercise more dangerous, especially if flame is involved, put the fan on the floor away from the burners, and let it run on low. Just moving the air in the room will help some. Latex-free gloves are a must in a lab for girls.

(Continued)

(Continued)

✓ Have girls observe the world before you introduce new information. This gives them a chance to begin to collect data to describe the larger picture. Before we started a unit on meteorology, I had my students keep a cloud diary. For two weeks, they were to watch and describe the clouds each day noting what the weather was. When we started the unit, the girls had a lot of information to bring to the unit and, usually, already had many questions.

✓ Distraction will help as well, and that is why many labs have music playing in the background. The music should be low so that the students have no trouble hearing your directions, but simply having something to listen to may help girls pay less attention to what is bothering them.

WHY GIRLS SHOULD DO WELL IN SCIENCE

We have spent a good deal of time examining the reasons that girls may not be interested or may do poorly in science. Are there reasons why girls might do well in science? There are a few reasons, and you should point these out to your students.

Study Skills

One of the best things about teaching girls is that almost all of them will do what was assigned. The research is very clear that girls are much better at planning and attention and are somewhat better at successive processing than boys (Naglieri & Rojahn, 2001). Here, planning refers to behaviors involved in managing and regulating behavior; for example, deciding what you are going to do before you do it. Attention refers to behaviors involved in being alert to the environment and resisting distractions. Successive processing refers to behaviors involved in accepting, evaluating, and retaining information. These skills are necessary for paying attention to what the teacher asks, being able to process the information and remember it, and motivating oneself to do the work that is asked. True, these skills are advantageous in all courses. They are particularly important in science because the best students do more than just learn the material; they are able to see how the material relates to the larger world and be able to apply it in novel situations (Feist, 2006).

Self-Discipline

Part of study skills is completing assigned tasks, and girls have been shown to be more self-disciplined and therefore more likely to do homework (Duckworth & Seligman, 2006). Being prepared for a laboratory exercise will help a student understand what is happening, and most girls are usually prepared. Again, this is an advantage in all courses, but girls will work even in courses they don't like, so the teacher has a better chance of grabbing a girl's attention because she will do the work. Eventually, she may find that she actually does like the course.

One problem that occurs every now and then arises out of girls' need to please adults. If their results do not agree with what they expected to get or with what other members of the class got, some girls may get upset because they see their results as an indication of failure. Make sure that you point out to all students, at every chance, that science is not about finding what you expected to find; it is about finding what happens in front of you. If that doesn't agree with everyone else, it may mean that you are wrong, or it may mean that everyone else is wrong. They also need to understand that science is not exact and that there is an acceptable variation in results. Science requires honesty in reporting results, and success is not getting the expected answer but in describing what actually happened.

SUGGESTIONS FOR APPLYING THE THEORY TO YOUR CLASSROOM

✓ Give students directions for laboratory exercises the day before. Girls are likely to come to class prepared for the exercise and, therefore, will feel more confident.

✓ Be careful not to let girls get entrenched in one particular style for laboratory reports. Make sure that you require different types of reports. I have taught girls who got very upset when I asked for a different approach to a report because it did not follow the style they had used for another teacher. These four questions will help frame a report for all levels of students:

  o What were the questions posed by the laboratory exercise?
  o What information was gathered that answered or failed to answer those questions?
  o What is the best way to report the information so that someone who was not there can understand what was done, why it was done, and what happened?
  o Why did you get the results you did?

✓ One problem that girls have in preparing lab reports is that they may be more comfortable with a narrative style, and the result can be much longer than the account needs to be.

  o Require that students turn in an outline of a lab report first so that they can be sure of what information should be included and what should not.
  o Usually materials and procedures are listed in a report so that a minimum amount of description is included. Some girls will need you to assure them that style is correct, as they will try to write you a story about what they did.
  o If the discussion part of the report is too involved, have the student present her points in a numbered or bulleted list.

(Continued)

(Continued)

✓ Frequently, have a class discussion on why various groups get different results. Have students calculate and examine acceptable differences in results.

o Have students keep track of all of their results. Over time, it is likely that they will find that their answers will be both above and below the expected values.

o Guide the class discussion to focus on why not every group got the same answer, what were some of the variables, and what could they have done to reduce the chance of variation.

o Assign students to report on famous mistakes in science; penicillin is a well-known example.

WHAT CAN BE DONE TO HELP?

Even though girls have the skills to do well in science, many are going to need some assistance to believe that they can succeed.

Encouragement and Mentors

The one factor most often mentioned to encourage girls successfully to enter the sciences is early exposure to programs designed just for them together with the support of female mentors. There are a many great programs available for girls that report improvement in girls' interest in and knowledge of science (Rahm & Moore, 2005; Yanowitz & Vanderpool, 2004). You will find a list of science programs just for girls, with the list of engineering programs in Chapter 8.

All of these programs provide interface with scientific inquiry and activities as well as support by mentors. In many cases, the mentors are females who are practicing scientists or engineers, and in some cases, the mentors are female academics or older students. In all cases, following such programs, girls report that they have increased interest in and knowledge about the various areas around which the programs are based (Ferreira, 2001; Hammrich, 1998).

Methods to Change Girls' Minds

A great deal of the difficulty girls have with science is because their perception of what scientists do is rather negative. They just don't believe that they would like science. They will agree that biology may be interesting because it involves animals and plants, but probably not physics. Many girls and their families still believe that science is something that is more suitable for boys and that wanting to become a scientist is not characteristic of a girl. That attitude is changing, but the process is rather slow.

Introduce Early

All of the reasons for introducing math early also apply here. Additionally, the sooner you can bring scientists into the classroom to encourage girls to get interested in science the better. This does not mean that the scientist just comes to talk to the students; the scientist needs to work *with* the students on some project. All of the most successful programs that involve girls in STEM areas follow this pattern, making sure that the girls get to see the scientist in action as well as provide assistance. For suggestions, look at the programs on the various Web sites listed in Chapter 8 to see how the programs are designed.

One suggestion was made that the organizers of such programs should make sure that the female scientists who are the focus of the efforts are well versed in the reasons that girls may not be interested in science. The adults, even though they are women, may not be aware of the beliefs of your students about scientists and particularly about women scientists. Furthermore, if the message can be framed in a way to show the students how the particular science can be used to help people, the chance that the students will receive the message positively will be increased (Yanowitz & Vanderpool, 2004).

Work in Groups

Girls like to work in cooperative and collaborative groups, and you will see that all of the programs mentioned earlier do just that. Having girls work in small groups is a great way to introduce a new topic as girls derive support from one another.

What is interesting is that there is some indication that in a coed classroom, girls will do better in single-sex groups (Huguet & Régner, 2007). The observation was that in the mixed-sex groups the girls were less likely to speak up, and in the single-sex groups, they interacted more (Ding & Harskamp, 2006). It is the involvement in the lesson and in the exercise that increases the chance of any student learning science (Burkam, Lee, & Smerdon, 1997), and if girls are more likely to engage in the science exercise in single-sex groups, then that is how they will learn best.

Appeal to Their Interests

A problem will arise if the group has decided that science is not something they are going to be interested in. In this case, either you will have to find someone who can break through their disinterest or find something they are interested in that relates to your topic. The world is based on science, so it will not be as hard as you think. In the movie *Legally Blonde,* in the final courtroom scene, the character Elle Woods wins her court case by pointing out that the witness could not have taken a shower or she would have lost all of her permanent curls. What makes this so wonderful is that Elle is a stereotypical blonde-haired woman who authoritatively cites the complex chemistry involved in creating permanent waves as evidence for her argument. Do not demean girls' interests simply because they do not seem important or complex enough. The girl who starts by investigating which sun-protection product works best may end up developing a treatment for skin cancer.

Girls are more likely to become interested in science when it is introduced as material to investigate rather than as a demonstration to impress. The more girls have the chance to do real science, the more likely they are to see science positively. Make sure that your students begin to see themselves as working collaboratively toward a goal. Girls are very interested in the world around them, but less about the short-term showy demonstration and more about how they can use science to help them explain and predict what happens in their world (Cox & Fisher, 2008).

My first teaching position was in a girls' school where I taught general science and life science among other classes. The school was in Virginia close to Washington, DC, and we had many museums to provide examples for our lessons.

SUGGESTIONS FOR APPLYING THE THEORY TO YOUR CLASSROOM

✓ When the general science class covered geology, we took a field trip to the Smithsonian to look at all the gems and minerals in the Museum of Natural History. We used the Hope diamond to study crystal structure—it is large enough to see the structure and it was recut to try to change the bad luck associated with it; its present structure is fascinating. Because diamonds are not actually cut but rather split along their crystal structure, it was a great example for the lesson. You might find a local jeweler who will come and discuss crystal structure in gemstones.

✓ We constructed simple spectroscopes using oatmeal boxes and inexpensive diffraction grids, which are easily found in scientific equipment sources. We used a variety of different light sources including fluorescent bulbs, grow lights, incandescent bulbs, candle flames, and neon lights. The girls were fascinated by the colors that were produced by different light sources. I asked the art teacher to come talk about how different light sources made surfaces look different. We took color photographs and compared the difference in appearance of the same person in different lights, and we discussed why people tend to look green under fluorescent lights. Using information from the spectroscopes, the girls predicted what wavelengths of light needed to be added to the light source to make people look better in a photograph. Again, an exhibit at the Smithsonian showed similar information.

✓ Photography is a combination of art and science and, these days, technology, with the advent of digital cameras.

  o The first step may be using the paper available in science equipment catalogs that allows you to put an object on the paper and expose it to light. When the paper is developed, what appears is a white figure on blue paper.

  o Invite a photographer to show your class the art of taking pictures and the knowledge of optics required to expose film.

  o You might also include a lesson on developing film, which will introduce chemistry.

✓ If you are not close to a science museum, you can find a lot of visual information from the Web sites for the National Geographic, the Smithsonian, and your state science museum or children's museum.

✓ Zoos and wildlife rehabilitation centers usually have outreach programs to bring animals to schools. In addition, most colleges and universities have programs to send professors or graduate students to schools with demonstrations of various phenomena—just call the appropriate department and ask if they can help you or know someone who can. You may also be able to go to the Web site for that part of the university and find a description of the types of school programs that their faculty will provide.

✓ To help the girls learn to read maps, I obtained United States Geological Survey (USGS) maps of their neighborhoods and we pinpointed their houses, the school, the boys' school nearby, and other interesting features. Because the girls all lived in an urban area, I also got maps from other places that I thought they might be interested in, such as a popular beach area, the ski resort where some went in the winter, and the rural area where I grew up. You can get copies from http://topomaps.usgs.gov/.

✓ Girls who live in urban areas or who have not traveled much need exposure to maps and geography. Developing orienteering courses in your building or on your campus are a good way for girls to get a sense of space and direction.

✓ The life science class and I visited the National Zoo where we were given a special tour looking at camouflage and how animals protect themselves with color. If there is a national guard or service facility near you, there may be someone who can come talk about how the armed forces use camouflage.

✓ A group of birding enthusiasts was happy to come to school and give my students basic information about identifying birds. One individual was very good at mimicking birdcalls, which interested some of the students.

✓ When we studied plants, I asked for help from the local floral shop, and they gave me many flowers that they could not use. We dissected the flowers, and the students drew pictures of the various parts of the flowers. Then we compared the parts of the flowers, and the girls figured out that the flowers mostly came in two categories—corresponding to monocots and dicots.

(Continued)

(Continued)

✓ The mother of one of the students came and gave a talk about the genetics aspects of her dog breeding business. She brought pictures of the parents and their puppies so the girls could see some of the traits for which she was trying to breed.

✓ Chromatography is something most girls are interested in, as they are fascinated to see what colors are used to make other colors. Get thick coffee filters or filter paper from your chemistry department and cut the filters in long strips with a point on the end. These strips should be suspended from a straightened paper clip over the mouth of a glass or jar that is at least four to five inches high (see Figure 5.2). The tip of the strip should be slightly immersed in a little water in the bottom. Before putting the strip in the jar, the student should select a water-based marker and draw a thick line across the strip about a half inch above the point. When the strip is placed in the container, the water will move up the strip and the different colors that are used to make the marker will separate. Students are usually fascinated to see that green markers have blue and yellow in them. Inexpensive black markers have interesting results as well. Suspend strips marked with permanent markers in both water and either fingernail polish remover or acetone to show students that the reason markers are permanent is just that the ink does not dissolve in water.

Figure 5.2 Chromotography Setup

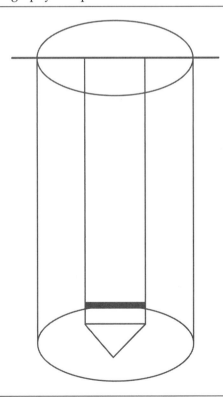

**SUGGESTIONS FOR APPLYING
THE THEORY TO YOUR CLASSROOM**

✓ *CSI* and *Mythbusters*, both TV shows that focus on applied science and feature women scientists, have accompanying materials for teachers. One unit linked to *CSI* involves the use of insects to determine various facts about crime scenes. A link to this unit can be found at www.lawrencehallofscience.org. The Discovery Channel Web site devoted to *Mythbusters* has video clips, lesson plans, and activities linked to the show, which can be found at http://school .discoveryeducation.com/teachers/myth-busters/.

✓ PBS has similar Web sites to accompany the many science shows that can be found there.

Although I recommend that you slant science experiences toward girls' interests, only do so long enough to get girls interested in the subject. I noticed that the pair of girls in a summer Lego robotics program had the best-looking robot. However, they were also having more success getting their robot properly programmed to complete the path because they were being more careful and listening to each other's suggestions. They may have started by making sure that their robot looked good, but they were also very interested in and succeeding at the technology.

Along with robotics, rocketry and flight are typically topics that have not interested many girls. However, such programs as the Sally Ride Science Camps have had great success in these areas by providing opportunities for girls to be involved in these areas with women as team leaders. Remember from the material at the beginning, astronomy has long been an area that women are interested in and where they are gaining in numbers.

Reality Projects

For all of the reasons that reality projects work in math, they are even better in science. We have discussed using examples from real life to illustrate the lessons of your students, but reality projects require students to become involved in a topic, not merely observe science in the laboratory. The summer camps and other programs designed to interest girls in science use that approach with great results. Research has shown that students learn science best when they are an active part of the lab exercise and not just observers (Burkam et al., 1997).

When talking with an older friend about this book, she said that there was no hope for her in math and science when she was in school and she wished me luck. She is an accomplished tailor who makes beautiful clothes, and I pointed out that she had to have exceptional skills in geometry and spatial relationships to create her clothes, especially because I know she rarely uses a pattern. She looked a little dubious, and I went on to explain that if she really had no skills in this area, she would be unable to take flat pieces of cloth and turn them into three-dimensional clothing, particularly because she was so good at matching stripes and other patterns in the fabric. She said that she had no trouble making clothing because she had the evidence for her decisions in front of her. I pointed out that what she was doing was similar to the reality projects that I recommended to help girls use reality to learn math and science.

There are innumerable projects that you can devise for your students, but you can get your students to develop their own. In my high school science classes, I made each student write down three topics or facts that interested her in the material we had covered so far. Then I sat down with each student and we figured out the student's project together. None of the projects required specialized equipment and all could be done either at school or at home.

One student used small houseplants to determine which of part of commercial fertilizer did the best job helping the plants to grow. Another student, using a calorimeter apparatus built from a soda can, did an exhaustive caloric analysis of the food in the cafeteria. She was trying to show the administration that the food offered to the girls was too high in calories. A middle school student in my physical science class was interested in the different acoustic properties of various woods. She was a violinist and worked with a luthier to investigate which woods were likely to produce better tones. Another student was interested in the effect of color on taste and obtained small cubes of potatoes, radishes, turnips, cauliflowers, onions, and other white vegetables. The subjects were offered the cubes in their native white state, dyed pink, and dyed blue. She and her subjects were fascinated that no one could correctly identify food when it was dyed blue. You will find specific instructions for how to frame these projects at the end of Chapter 6. Those directions are there because this technique is an excellent way to get girls interested in science in a coed class.

What makes these projects different from traditional lab exercises?

- Each student or group of students in a class does a different exercise.
- The students develop the exercises based on their own experience or on a question that they have.
- Because each exercise is unique, the students have to do some individual research to help them shape the project so that the results answer their question.
- Depending on the level of the students, they will work somewhat independently. Third-grade students would develop a precise order of operations with the teacher who would supervise to make sure that everything was going well. Eleventh-grade students would submit to the teacher a proposed protocol for review and provide periodic reports on their progress.

- At the conclusion of the projects, each student writes an independent analysis of the project and presents the results to the class for their scrutiny. If the project was a joint venture, the students will give a joint presentation. Younger students might take pictures of their projects at the beginning and at the end to show to the class or provide some graphic representation of their results. Older students might accompany visual documentation with a written account of their progress.
- Because the class does a variety of projects, the whole class can cover much more material because all students present their results to the class.

SCIENCE AND GIRLS

The numbers of girls involved in science is growing, but not very rapidly. Girls like to work together on projects, a method that is ideally suited for science laboratory exercises. Connecting what happens in the lab to what happens in the world will interest girls in science.

ANSWERS TO QUIZ

1. A—Girls enrolled in more biology or AP biology courses. In high school that year, 93.7% of girls took regular biology compared to 90.8% of boys. The difference for AP biology is similar, and more girls (18%) took those courses compared to boys (13.9%) (U.S. Department of Education [U.S. DoE], National Center for Education Statistics, 2007).

2. A—Girls, in 2005, took more courses in chemistry than boys, 69.7% compared to 62.5%. The difference is similar in the upper-level courses: 8.6% of girls compared to 7.6% of boys (U.S. DoE, 2007).

3. B—Boys enrolled in more physics courses than girls. The difference was not as great as you might think; 34.8% of boys and 30.8% of girls took physics. In AP courses, the relationship is the same: 6.6% of boys compared to 4.1% of girls (U.S. DoE, 2007).

4. B—Boys took more courses in biology, chemistry, and physics, based on the preceding statistics, but not many more. While 28.2% of boys took all three sciences, so did 26.5% of girls.

5. C—An equal number of girls and boys who took the SAT took physics courses (College Board, 2006).

(Continued)

(Continued)

6. A—Women, in 2004, received 62% of bachelor degrees in biological sciences. The same year, 20.5% of bachelor degrees in engineering went to women, the lowest in all the science fields (National Science Foundation, 2007).

7. A—Women receiving bachelor degrees in computer science dropped from 28.5% in 1995 to 25% in 2004. This was the only math and science field that showed a drop for women (National Science Foundation, 2007).

8. A—Women are more likely to have a job requiring the use of a computer, 61.8% of women use a computer compared to 49.9% of men (U.S. Census Bureau, 2006). Of course, many of those positions are secretarial, traditionally a female occupation.

9. B—Men are employed in computer and mathematics areas a great deal more than women. Only 27% of employees in the computer and mathematics occupations are women (U.S. Bureau of Labor Statistics, 2006)

10. B—Men were employed as veterinarians more than girls. In 2004, 38.7% of veterinarians were women, but in the same year, 74.5% of individuals receiving doctor of veterinary medicine degrees were women (U.S. Bureau of Labor Statistics, 2006; Snyder et al., 2006).

6

Teaching Math and Science to Girls in a Coed School

SOURCE: Photographer: Duane Berger. Used with permission.

A lthough teaching math and science to girls in a single-sex environment allows the teacher to focus approaches toward specific learning capacities, the fact is that most schools are not single sex. So what are the issues that may affect how girls view math and science, and what problems, if any, exist that may make it harder for girls to learn math and science in a coed environment? What are strategies that the teacher in a coed class can use to improve the chances that girls will enjoy and do well in math and science?

SOCIOCULTURAL ISSUES

History

A century ago, science and math (to a lesser extent) were considered courses that were appropriate for girls to study and in which they did well. For a variety of reasons, that attitude changed, so by the late 1960s, science and math were considered harder for girls. The attitude is reversing, but it is a slow process.

SUGGESTIONS FOR APPLYING THE THEORY TO YOUR CLASSROOM

✓ Introduce all students to famous women scientists and mathematicians by telling students stories, giving them biographies to read, or having them produce research reports about women in the past.

✓ Introduce all students to present-day women scientists and mathematicians by inviting these women to your classroom, having them do projects with the students, or having the students visit these women in their laboratories. Not only will this help girls but it will also help boys learn that math and science are not exclusively in the masculine domain.

Families

Even after years of educators talking about the problem of girls in science, technology, engineering, and math (STEM) courses and many programs to help girls do better, families still emerge as a sizable part of the reasons girls don't believe that math and science are suitable for them.

SUGGESTIONS FOR APPLYING THE THEORY TO YOUR CLASSROOM

✓ Invite families to your classroom to observe the presentation of reality projects. This is especially good if one family member is a mathematician, scientist, or uses math or science in his or her job. However, if a child has a family member who is a mathematician or scientist, please make sure that neither you nor the family assumes that the child will be interested in or good at those subjects. My father taught foreign languages and was fluent in French; my mother taught English and was a published author. I flunked French three times and frequently received D's in English. However, I usually made A's in my math and science classes, which totally mystified them.

✓ If the problem is that families don't believe that girls can do well in math and science, invite women who are in the STEM careers to come and speak to the parents and to the students. I realize that, usually, the family members who come to these programs are already convinced, but getting the information out will help. This will also provide some evidence to all that math and science are not exclusively male domains.

✓ Include family members in the reality projects as experts. If a child is trying to figure out how much it will cost to repaint her room, she may want to compare whether it is more economical to paint with one coat of the expensive paint versus two coats of the inexpensive paint. This student can interview a fellow student's family member who owns a hardware store, who is a building contractor, or who is an interior decorator as part of the process of collecting information necessary for making the decision about which type of paint to use. Younger students can write a list of questions and send them home with the fellow student; older students can e-mail or interview the family member over the telephone or in person.

✓ One caveat for this exercise: It is entirely possible that the adult whose expertise is necessary to complete the project will try to do the work for the girl. Develop a set of guidelines for the adults so that they only answer questions or provide information and do not do any of the work. This is especially true for science fair projects. As a former science fair judge, I was frequently tempted to give the parent the award. The advantage of reality projects, as outlined here, is that the student must present her report to the class. Questions from the class will uncover how well the student understands her topic.

Other Teachers

Even though they may be unaware of doing so, teachers in other courses may reinforce the notion that math and science are not for girls through indirect statements and stereotypical remarks.

SUGGESTIONS FOR APPLYING THE THEORY TO YOUR CLASSROOM

✓ Encourage your administration to provide professional-development programs that will introduce your colleagues to the notion that girls can do well in science and math. What you may find is that some teachers are made so uneasy by

(Continued)

(Continued)

talking about STEM courses that they won't even listen to a lecture on how well girls can do in these subjects. You might suggest that the head of your department take these teachers aside privately to encourage them to come to the program, not because they will be asked to do math or science, but because it is important that they acquire the skills to support the efforts of other teachers to encourage girls.

✓ Involve teachers of other subjects in class projects. The science teacher can invite the art teacher to discuss how oil paints are made, the history teacher to discuss the origins of the industrial revolution, or the coach to discuss the physics of hitting a ball with a tennis racquet. The math teacher can invite the music teacher to show the relationship of math to music, the bookkeeper to show how double-entry books are kept, or the librarian to show how the school catalogs the books. Even the language arts teacher can come by to talk about science fiction or biographies of famous mathematicians.

✓ One popular program is *writing across the curriculum*. Encourage the faculty to get involved in teaching students how to write differently for different subjects. This is an area where some girls will shine, and by writing about STEM topics, they may change their minds about how they feel about the subjects. Although I found it difficult to write an essay for my English teacher, I had no trouble writing lab reports for biology and chemistry. Knowing I could write in one area gave me confidence to keep trying in other areas. My classmates with excellent skills in language arts found that although they had trouble with the more computational or detailed sections of science, they could more easily write essays describing what happened.

ROLE MODELS

We have mentioned, several times, the importance of providing appropriate role models for girls, but please, remember that just inviting someone to come and talk to your class is not enough; the students need to interact with the expert for the role model to be successful. These role models are also very important for boys who may not be acquainted with successful women engineers or physicists.

SUGGESTIONS FOR APPLYING THE THEORY TO YOUR CLASSROOM

✓ Internships and shadowing are good ways for girls with particular interests to have a close relationship with an appropriate role model. If boys are given an opportunity to interact with women mathematicians and scientists, they may change their ideas about the gendered nature of those areas. The scope of careers is wide open here. You will find the state-level professional organizations a great help in contacting appropriate practitioners.

o Science-related careers include individuals who are farmers, chefs or others involved in food preparation, research chemists, meteorologists, pharmacists, nurses, doctors, veterinarians, and other health professionals.

o Technology-related careers include individuals who are computer programmers, computer hardware or software technicians, Webmasters, AutoCAD designers, technical writers, information-systems managers, and multimedia artists.

o Engineering-related careers include individuals who are civil engineers (private or public practice), surveyors, architects, sound technicians, astronomers, and computer engineers.

o Math-related careers include individuals who are insurance agents, certified public accountants, stockbrokers, financial analysts, small-business owners, market researchers, and statisticians.

✓ School-sponsored career days are only good if the students get to talk with the experts. Do not simply invite people to come to speak to the whole school from the front of the auditorium, as students who are not good auditory learners will not get much from the presentation. It will also help if the invited guests are graduates of your school—that adds a personal note, which will interest both boys and girls.

✓ As part of the writing-across-the-curriculum program, students can write about personal interviews with appropriate experts or write a biography of a famous female mathematician or scientist. The biography will require some research and you might require that the student provide an example of the work done by the subject of the biography.

VERBAL VERSUS VISUAL APPROACH

We have discussed, at length, that girls usually approach a subject through the verbal lens. When I teach girls, I always start by either assigning some material to be read or by discussing the topic, and usually I do both. When I teach boys, I never assign reading material before we have had a chance to investigate the material in the laboratory, even briefly. How do you put those two disparate approaches together?

The important thing is not to depend exclusively on one approach or the other. If you are teaching a coed class, certainly begin with written or oral presentations. Remember, however, that children do not learn just because you told them. Make sure that you combine verbal material with visual as well as offering chances for the students to practice what is being taught. To make sure that you reach as many students as possible, have some sort of visual display to accompany the words with which you begin the lesson. In math, generally the problem will serve as the display. If you are working on word problems, project the problems in a way that you can "box the operator." I enlarge the problem and copy it onto an acetate sheet for an overhead projector. Then I can write on the sheet with water-soluble markers. If you have a tablet-type computer, which is projected onto a screen, students can use the stylus to highlight on the screen. If you have a SMART Board, students can highlight directly on the board.

In science, prepare charts or use pictures or other graphics to help illustrate the information in your lecture. One of the reasons that visual students usually have less trouble in Grades K–3 is that teachers in those grades are very aware of the necessity of presenting information in as many ways as possible because children are still learning to read. In the later grades, when the emphasis shifts to reading to learn, some teachers will primarily rely on oral or written presentations, and that may not be the best way to engage some students.

Lecture is one of the primary ways that I present information to my students, but I am aware that students lose focus after a while. All students will need some sort of break, some sooner than others. I shift gears by asking questions, by asking for the students' opinion on the material we are discussing, by taking a detour through related material (my students believe that they are getting me off track, but I always tie it in to the material at hand), or by engaging in an activity. Girls tend to be less obviously restless, especially when compared to boys. However, they are probably just quieter about it and may be daydreaming or engaging in some other off-task activity. In a coed classroom, be careful not to spend too much time describing what students are to do, as you may lose the attention of the more restless students. Make sure that you have copies of the directions to hand out to the students who need the words to be sure that all students understand what they are to do.

I cannot emphasize enough the need for the teacher to talk as little as possible in the science classroom.

SUGGESTIONS FOR APPLYING THE THEORY TO YOUR CLASSROOM

✓ I give the directions verbally and hand out a written version. I do not repeat myself. Yes, many students will not get the information the first time, but if I go over the directions, there are still students who have not understood what I have asked them to do. At some point, I have to move on. Shortly, students will catch on to the fact that you don't repeat yourself, and they will pay better attention while you are talking. This technique is designed for high school students. In the lower grades, I might repeat the directions, but only once. If students know that you will repeat the directions, they won't listen.

✓ Start the exercise. Those who were listening or who will read the directions will get to work. Those who have not gotten the information will need your assistance. This is the place to teach them how to find out what to do for themselves.

   o Many girls want your assurance that what they are doing is correct. They need confidence building. Tell them to start doing what they think is right and you will check with them as soon as all the rest of the students are at work. Remind them that they need to learn to work on their own.

   o Many boys will not pay attention because they know that the teacher will give them the information again. Hand them directions as diagrams, if appropriate, and ask them what they think they are to do. If they are working in a way that is not exactly what you wanted but is on task, leave them alone. Either they will arrive at the correct answer or they will not. If they do, that may be a good way for them to learn. If they do not, that will tell them that they need to do it your way in the future. I know that teachers are very concerned that every child has the same lab experience. You cannot guarantee that in any case, and teaching students to be self-reliant does not take a great deal of time at the beginning of a course. If you don't have to repeat yourself, you save a tremendous amount of class time.

   o In a coed class, do not try to get all students working in the same way at the same time. Students need to approach the learning process from their cognitive strengths, and there may be as many different ways of learning as there are students in the room. In a single-sex class, you can make some assumptions about common learning approaches, but not all girls learn the same way, and you will need to help some students approach the lesson from another point of view.

Girls are less willing to move around a classroom, as they can find the movement distracting; boys, on the other hand, require movement. It is possible to have movement and respect girls' need for a minimum of disturbances. The best method is to have regulations about how students move—quietly, going quickly to the next area—and having the material well structured so that when students get to the next area, they know what is expected of them and are ready to do it.

SUGGESTIONS FOR APPLYING THE THEORY TO YOUR CLASSROOM

✓ Make sure that your stations are well separated in the classroom and that there are clear pathways between the desks so that students are not tempted to shove desks as they move around the classroom.

(Continued)

(Continued)

✓ Even though each student may have a worksheet that describes what she or he is to do at each station, remind the students to look at the sheet. Post a sign with directions such as, "Station 3: Read the directions for this station from your sheet and answer Questions 5, 6, and 7 after you have completed the activity."

✓ Provide a place where worksheets are to be returned when finished. This reduces the questions such as, "What are we to do with this when we are finished?" Yes, students will ask that question at the beginning of the year, but they will get used to the routine and, eventually, simply place the sheets where they belong.

✓ Have on hand a quiet at-desk activity ready for any students who finish early. This is a perfect place for one of the logic puzzles or a game of chess.

Remember that girls are less likely to be visual in their academic approach and may have trouble grasping information if the only source is the class exercise. Help them learn to take notes on what happens so that they may have an accurate record to refer to. Remember, also, that girls are less likely to get involved with activities where material is manipulated, so make sure that they are encouraged to do that. If you are not careful, the boys will dominate the lab exercise and girls will be further convinced science is not for them.

SUGGESTIONS FOR APPLYING THE THEORY TO YOUR CLASSROOM

✓ All students need to learn to take notes, and science class is an excellent place to learn, as there are specific facts that can be easily checked.

✓ If you regularly divide students for group work, one of the problems is that some students always take the same job in the exercise. Identify each task by a particular number. Number 1 could be the person who reads the directions and keeps track of what is being done. Number 2 is the person who writes down the results, and Number 3 is the person who actually does the exercise. Then, as students are selected for a group, they can draw a number to see what job they will do. That way, all students have an equal chance at learning to do every task.

✓ If you have a girl in your science class who is particularly reluctant to engage in a lab exercise, take her aside to find out if she is overwhelmed by the other students, if she does not understand what she is to do, or if she does not like to learn through manipulating materials. Help her deal with her difficulty, but do not excuse her from participating. If you believe the lab exercise is important, all students should participate.

SINGLE-SEX CLASSES OR PROGRAMS

I know I promised that I would provide examples of strategies to help girls with math and science in a coed environment, but the research is strong that single-sex programs or classes in coed schools can be very beneficial. Don't forget, almost all of the summer programs and camps that were mentioned earlier are single sex. All of the research that follows involves single-sex classes inside coed schools and some inside a coed class. I am aware that some schools will not allow you to do this, and I can only suggest that you show the research to the person responsible for making that decision. If you are able to persuade your school to allow single-sex classes or groups, students may volunteer to participate.

One advantage for single-sex classes is the reduction in *stereotype threat* and in *sex stereotyping* of math and science. You will remember that stereotype threat is the belief that you will not be good at something just because of who you are. For example, boys may not try to read, as everyone knows they are not good at reading. Math is an area that has been identified as one place where stereotype threat is a problem for girls (Spencer, Steele, & Quinn, 1999). Girls may not be interested in science and math simply because they believe that most girls have trouble in these areas.

Girls who do participate in science may have an interest you can use to get them involved in class. One study noted that most of the girls taking a full science and math curriculum were interested in medical careers and that the improvement in the performance of women in science and math was, partially, because of positive progress in the admission of women to careers involved in the biological courses (McEwen, Knipe, & Gallagher, 1997). Another study concluded that girls in coed schools gained more from single-sex introductory physics classes that were oriented to their learning interests and styles than they did from a coed class. The reason given in this study was that the girls developed positive self-concepts about their abilities as students of physics (Hoffman, 2002).

Having a girl for a lab partner can help as well. In a coed physics laboratory, girls were likely to learn better when their lab partner was another girl than when the partner was a boy (Ding & Harskamp, 2006). More recently, a study agreed, finding that girls in single-sex math groups did much better than their cohorts in coed groups (Huguet & Régner, 2007). Even if your classes are coed, consider categorizing students by sex when forming groups to work together in class. And yes, I know that may create a situation where boys will believe that the reason for the groups is that the girls have trouble with science or math. The boys will find out that the girls are quite capable when students present their results to the class. You may also find out that when girls work together they are more willing to speak up in a coed class than they might have if they worked with a boy.

During the middle school years, the problem of getting the *right* answer for girls is most acute. Research has shown that having girls work in same-sex groups reduces the focus on finding the right answer (Huguet & Régner, 2007), so if this gets to be a problem, have girls work on problem sets in same-sex groups. As math becomes more complicated, have all students develop alternative solution paths. That may be more difficult for girls who are searching for the one true method to make sure they have the right answer. In same-sex groups, girls are likely to be a bit bolder about trying alternative solutions.

Computer science is one of the few areas where the percentage of women graduating with bachelor degrees has decreased. In 1995, 28.5% of bachelor degrees were awarded to women, and in 2006, only 20.6% were awarded to women (U.S. Department of Education, National Center for Education Statistics, 2007). Girls, in one study, were more satisfied with the environment and teaching in a single-sex computer class than in a coed class (Logan, 2007). The point was made that, in a single-sex classroom, the teacher can use strategies that are designed to meet the needs of particular students, and given the information about gender differences in learning, a single-sex class might best meet the needs of all students in these technical areas.

A report about an after-school technical program with some single-sex groups described that the students were more interested in single-sex groups than were the teachers. The reasons the teachers gave for preferring coed groups included that they were more fun and easier to manage—the girls were cooperative and the boys more interested in the activity, so they did most of the work (Salminen-Karlsson, 2007). Remember, what the teacher and the students experience are not necessarily similar, and this program is a good example. This same report cautioned that although the girls preferred the single-sex groups and appeared to learn a great deal from them, in single-sex groups the boys continued to stereotype technical activities as being part of the male domain.

The problem is that many girls respond well to single-sex math and science classes, primarily because the class is focused on their learning strengths and interests. On the other hand, in single-sex classes two things may happen: Boys may strengthen their beliefs that science and math are boy courses, and girls may find it difficult to compete with boys when they get to a coed situation. As a science teacher, I find it much easier to teach science in a single-sex environment before the 10th grade because of the different learning styles. In a girls' school, the first day of my introductory physical science class starts with a discussion about the course—what it will be about and what they can expect to be doing. As we get into the course, I always give them the lab sheets to take home the night before a lab exercise so that they can read them and be familiar with what they are going to be asked to do the next day. With older students, a coed class is less of a problem as the students are beginning to approach learning from similar directions.

If you do institute single-sex groups in your classes, be sensitive to the possibility that this may encourage boys to feel superior to girls. Students may also develop a competitive edge, which if friendly is fine, but if the girls perform better than the boys do, this can result in girls downplaying their successes and boys downplaying the importance of the lesson. Changing the assignment of students in groups will help, even if the groups are single-sex, as students will not form alliances, which can develop the "us-against-them" attitudes.

Whether or not you implement single-sex math and science courses will depend on the level of your students and the climate of your school. This style of class will fit well in some areas and not in others. However, in middle school, if you have the chance to try single-sex classes, I encourage you to do so; what happens may surprise you. You can get help from the National Association for Single-Sex Public Education (www.singlesexschools.org) or from local single-sex schools.

PRACTICAL APPLICATIONS

Several times, I have suggested practical applications of both math and science as excellent methods of getting girls involved. These come under the heading of "reality projects" and can be *virtual* or *actual*. In the past, science and math were interesting because children came in contact with applications on a daily basis. As our technology gets more complicated, students become somewhat removed from the actual use of science and math, which can then take on somewhat mythic proportions. Adults are frequently surprised at the facility that small children have on computers. They just start pushing buttons, and if something bad happens, they just start over again. Adults somehow have come to believe that they have to understand how a computer functions to use it. This is typified by the remark, "If something goes wrong, I don't know how to fix it." I ask them if they have any idea how many computers are in their automobiles. Most people don't, and I am sure they don't know how to fix those, but that doesn't keep them from driving.

Children used to have chores to do that required them to be totally responsible for some aspect of family life. Not only did this provide children with a venue to solve problems with no help from adults, but this also gave them intimate knowledge of how various things worked. For example, children knew how a woodstove worked, how plants react to water (or lack of it), what happens to animals when they aren't fed on time, and the effect of a diluted solution of white vinegar on glass (gets the glass very clean). Children were also allowed to play without adult supervision. Deciding the rules of the game and pacifying the owner of the ball so she or he would not go home developed negotiating and problem-solving skills.

Many high school students have jobs that they *need* to support their automobiles, their collection of electronic devices, and/or their wardrobe. Although there is great benefit in students learning to be responsible and reliable, which they will probably learn if they are good employees, most jobs for teenagers don't require many skills. For example, they don't have to do mental math, as the cash register does all of that for them.

If students don't have some way to see the practical applications of science and math, they are not likely to find the connections between these subjects and their own life. When you point out that calculus can be used to discover the maximum speed a vehicle can attain under certain circumstances or the growth of money in a hedge fund, you can get students' attention. Understanding that cooking is chemistry and a bit of biology, for example, may help students take those subjects more seriously. Boys and girls can work together or not on these projects, as they choose. Because these are based on how science and math are used in everyday life, a coed approach is certainly more reasonable, especially for high-school-age students.

SUGGESTIONS FOR APPLYING THE THEORY TO YOUR CLASSROOM

✓ Make sure that reality projects are designed to meet the competency levels of your students, remembering that you can vary the requirements depending on a student's ability. Differentiated instruction is a technique that works well, and this is an excellent place to require different levels of performance from your students. A single grading rubric that is applied to all projects will make the assessment process equitable.

✓ One important facet of reality projects is that each student or group of students is doing something different. This way, when students report on their project to the whole class, the class covers more topics than if all did the same project. Some teachers have found that other members of the class do not pay attention to student presentations. One way around this is to have a few items on the next test come from those presentations or to have students turn in brief synopses of each presentation.

✓ For younger students, do not do all the presentations on one day. They will pay better attention when one or two groups of students per class present their findings at a time.

✓ Each student or group of students must present their findings to the whole class. This should be a somewhat formal process; it might involve a PowerPoint presentation or a poster session, where all students stand in front of a poster summarizing their results and answering questions of people who pass by. The attendees to the poster session can be other faculty, administrators, parents, and other students. Some students, many of them girls, may find it difficult to stand in front of the class and present their findings, and the poster session format avoids that. Speaking to a group is a common phobia, and having the chance to do this in a safe environment, such as a class, will help. It will also help introduce the younger students to the idea of presenting data.

✓ The sky is the limit when it comes to reality projects, and any list I provide might reduce the number of options you come up with. However, you may find it instructive to see how to phrase a project.

  ○ For Young Students

    ■ How big is your room? Measure the dimensions of your room and draw a diagram of the length, width, and height. (If the lesson involves studying early measurements, you can ask them to figure out how many feet—their feet—their room is, or how many hands.)

    ■ Can salt dissolve in every liquid? Obtain a number of liquids such as oil, vinegar, mouthwash, soda, and the like. Measure out the same amount of each liquid in a transparent container and put the same amount of salt in each and stir. Compare the solutions to find out if salt dissolves better in one of the liquids. Make sure you have an older family member to help you.

  ○ For Middle School Students

    ■ The school needs more parking, and there is an empty lot next to the present parking lot. You are to figure out how many cars would fit in the empty lot. Determine the area of the lot by measuring length and width. Search on the Internet for information about the standard size of a parking slot as well as the space required for backing the car out of the slot. You are to figure out the arrangement of parking places that allows the most cars to park and provide a diagram of what the parking lot will look like together with a cost estimate for paving the lot.

    ■ Can you really fry an egg on the sidewalk? You are to find out how hot a surface has to be to cook an egg in a reasonable amount of time—you decide what is reasonable—and whether or not an outside surface can get that hot. Time the process with a stopwatch, use a thermometer from the lab to determine how hot various surfaces get outside, and use an electric fry pan, with adult supervision, that can be set to the hottest temperature of an outside surface to determine if that is hot enough to cook the egg.

  ○ For Upper-Level Students

    ■ Computer passwords should, for best security, be eight digits long and at least one of the digits should be a letter and one should be a number. Why will this pattern do a good job of providing security? Show your work.

    ■ A man on the west coast floated in a lawn chair supported by a bunch of helium-filled balloons 200 miles from his starting point. If the man weighed 175 pounds, how many balloons would he need? You are welcome to use any type of balloon you can reasonably purchase, just make sure you include a description of it and where you might purchase the balloon. Don't forget that the lawn chair and the balloons have mass and that the composition of a balloon may allow very small molecules to escape. Make sure that you allow for expansion of your balloons remembering that the density of the atmosphere is greatest at the earth's surface. Your presentation should include a cost estimate for this experiment.

FINAL WORDS

Most girls use their verbal centers for memory, so make sure that you use words, both written and spoken, to introduce the material to your students. If a girl has problems with spatial relationships, remind her that cognitive skills continue to develop as we mature and her spatial skills will also improve. Allow all of your students to use a variety of techniques to solve problems; what works for you may not work for your students. If a student does not understand the most *elegant* solution but can get it in a much more laborious fashion, let the student struggle with the clumsier method. Once she understands where she is going, then she may be able to understand the simpler way.

Girls can do well in math and science, but you need to remember that some don't think they will and those around them may make it difficult for you to change their minds. In addition, although there has been a lot of progress, many careers are still not configured to allow women to progress and still be an active part of a family. You must also take into account the need of some girls to be involved in activities that involve interaction with others. As a teacher of math or science, you may have already made a similar decision. Encouraging girls in these areas and providing role models and practical applications will go a long way to keeping girls interested in the subjects. Remind your student that, although she may not like the study of math and science, these subjects impact our lives and a basic understanding of the principles is essential to living well. Also, know that you are a role model for your students and your attitude toward STEM courses will be very apparent to them. You may make a difference in a young woman's life. I would never have become a scientist if it were not for my math and science teachers. I hope you have that influence on one of your students.

7

Gendered Instruction

SOURCE: Photographer: Duane Berger. Used with permission.

There are three different ways schools offer gendered instruction: (1) coed schools where teachers are responsive to the different learning strengths and weaknesses of girls and boys, (2) coordinate schools where some classes in the school are coed and some of the classes are single-sex, and (3) single-sex schools where all the students are either girls or boys, including dual academies where the teachers teach only one gender. Whatever kind of school you teach in, the principles contained in this book can be applied in your classroom, even if you don't teach science or math.

Teachers ask for specific examples of how to include all students in their classes. What follows are suggestions using several well-known theories. First, I will briefly explain the theory and then give examples using what we know about how to teach the female brain. Remember that these theories can be considered lenses through which to view the instructional process. Some teachers have found these approaches helpful, and others have not, but they may suggest different ways to approach your students. These approaches are designed to help you implement the principles of teaching math and science to girls in coed classes. In each of the examples, activities specifically targeted for girls are in bold, but the lessons are designed for all students.

For public schoolteachers who need to see how the different components fit within national standards testing requirements, I have included a section of the Virginia Standards of Learning for middle-school life science. These standards conform to the national norms and are used here just as examples. You will find references to these particular standards in the sample lesson plans.

VIRGINIA STANDARDS OF LEARNING

Selected Standards of Learning, Commonwealth of Virginia

Life Science

Learning Standard (LS) 1: The student will plan and conduct investigations in which

- a. data are organized into tables showing repeated trials and means;
- b. variables are defined;
- c. metric units (International System of Units [SI]) are used;
- e. sources of experimental error are defined;
- f. dependent variables, independent variables, and constants are identified;
- g. variables are controlled to test hypotheses, and trials are repeated;
- i. interpretations from a set of data are evaluated and defended; and
- j. an understanding of the nature of science is developed and reinforced.

LS 3: The student will investigate and understand that all living things show patterns of cellular organization. Key concepts include

    a. cells, tissues, organs, and systems; and
    b. life functions and processes of cells, tissues, organs, and systems (respiration, removal of wastes, growth, reproduction, digestion, and cellular transport).

LS 4: The student will investigate and understand that the basic needs of organisms must be met to carry out life processes. The key concept is

    a. plant needs (light, water, gases, and nutrients).

LS 6: The student will investigate and understand the basic physical and chemical processes of photosynthesis and its importance to plant and animal life. Key concepts include

    a. energy transfer between sunlight and chlorophyll;
    b. transformation of water and carbon dioxide into sugar and oxygen; and
    c. photosynthesis as the foundation of virtually all food webs.

SOURCE: Virginia Life Science Standards of Learning, http://www.doe.virginia.gov/go/Sols/science7.pdf.

DIFFERENTIATED INSTRUCTION

According to Tomlinson, "A differentiated classroom provides different avenues to acquiring content, to processing, or making sense of ideas, and to developing products so that each student can learn effectively" (Tomlinson, 2004b, p. 1). When you change how you present information and what you ask students to do in response to their individual needs, you are differentiating instruction. Using gender as a lens is a very accessible way of producing different instructional approaches. The theory is that one instructional strategy will not reach all learners because they all have different skills, strengths, and educational backgrounds. In my ninth-grade science class, I have students who want to know whether I prefer the data from the lab displayed in a graph or chart working with students who have never written a lab report before in their lives. The problem is how to teach those who have limited science-lab experience without boring the students who have been doing this for years. By providing instructional opportunities for each type of learner, all students can learn and will make progress in the same classroom.

At first, differentiated instruction can seem overwhelming to the teacher. After all, who has time to provide a variety of approaches for every lesson? The usual suggestion is to do one unit. See how that goes—what the successes are and what needs work. Then the following semester or even the following year, plan another lesson using this technique. Integrate the instructional plan into your teaching slowly, as you have time. Proponents of differentiated instruction believe that as teachers become more adept at thinking this way, they find it easier and easier to produce instructional opportunities for their students based on this design. Although the initial planning for instruction can seem time-consuming, the actual teaching becomes more straightforward because instruction becomes more efficient.

For teachers in high school, some of what follows may seem as if it does not apply to what you do in the classroom. Look at the examples to see how active lab exercises can be adapted for a more verbal learning style without losing the more kinesthetic learners or overwhelming the verbal learner. You may not want to do as many activities as are suggested in these plans, but think about how you can incorporate activities that are verbal and auditory together with activities that are visual and hands-on.

Components of Differentiated Instruction

The following are key components of differentiated instruction according to Tomlinson (2004a, 2004b) and Heacox (2002).

Qualitative Approach

Differentiated instruction offers each student several different ways to approach the learning process. Some students learn best from written material, others do better with hands-on activities. I differ the presentation of material by presenting, in every class, at least some lecture, giving visual representations of the material together with notes written on the overhead projector, and reading something about the topic. My students may get information from a lab exercise, from research on the Internet or the library, from working with a group of classmates on a project, or from ancillary materials that I share with them, as well as from their textbook.

Product

The product that the students present varies as well. Students may be asked to write a paper, give an oral report, put the material in a chart or graph, prepare a debate, design a game, draw pictures, solve puzzles, or write questions, just to name a few. There are many ways for students to demonstrate their mastery of the material, and tests are but one. For girls who may exhibit test anxiety, using some of these other products to demonstrate a student's mastery will help develop confidence, which is the best way to counteract anxiety.

Assessment

Assessment is an ongoing process in my classroom. My ninth graders have a daily opportunity to show their progress, while I may assess my twelfth graders only twice a week. I am not a proponent of pop quizzes because, for the most part, they seem to be used to uncover students who have not done their homework. There are better ways, such as having students turn in their homework—of course, that means the teacher *must* look at it and return it the *next day.* Why? We know from the theory of learning that reinforcement must be quick and positive for learning to take place. If a child turns in work, she needs to have your assessment of that work while she can still remember why she did what she did. If you return papers several days later, some children will look at their papers and won-der why they wrote those answers or be totally surprised at what they did write. That requires a little planning on your part to make sure that you don't end up with a paper from every one of your students at the same time. The other solution is to have peers check the papers. Collect all papers and then distribute them randomly so that each student's paper is checked by another member of the class.

The assessments I use may be as simple as asking questions during class or asking the students to respond to the chapter questions in their textbook. I frequently ask students to write a paragraph explaining one of the points we went over in class. That helps the student who says, "I understand when you discuss it in class, but then can't remember it on the test." In a ninth-grade math class, students may be asked, "What are the steps in solving a rate and distance word problem?" In a twelfth-grade English class, students may be asked, "Where does the title of the story we are reading come from?"

Multiple Approaches

Another key component of differentiated instruction is the use of var-ied instructional approaches, including reading, writing, building models, conducting debates, delivering reports, and the like. Material can be pre-sented to the whole class, to a small group, or to an individual. The com-bination of approaches is what makes differentiated instruction effective (Heacox, 2002; Tomlinson, 2004a, 2004b).

In Figure 7.1, you will find a sample differentiated instruction lesson plan for a seventh-grade life science unit about plants and how they func-tion. Typical of such plans, you will see that there is a chance for students of differing abilities to engage in a higher- or lower-level of work. Remember that the prize for being a very capable student should not be more work than the rest of the class. Instead, very capable students should have work that is more challenging. On the other end of the spectrum, the student who has trouble with the material should not be given less work, but work that is designed for her educational ability. Again, material that works well with most girls will be in bold type.

The theme in life science for this made-up unit is "Environmental Effects on the Growth of Plants—Can Plants Survive on Cola?" The class will use a wide variety of sources to find out how different substances affect the growth of simple houseplants. In the column marked "Additional

Figure 7.1 Differentiated Instruction Unit for Seventh-Grade Life Science

Purpose: To use basic principles to explore the effect of the environment on living organisms

Learning Standards (LS): Life Science, Grade 7 Standards of Learning addressed in this unit are the following:

   LS 1: Conduct investigations

   LS 3: Understand patterns of cellular organization

   LS 4: Understand basic needs of organisms to carry out life processes

   LS 6: Understand basic physical and chemical processes of photosynthesis

Learning Objectives: (1) Students will be able to plan and conduct investigations. (2) Students will investigate and understand that the basic needs of organisms must be met to carry out life processes. (3) Students will be able to investigate and understand the basic physical and chemical processes of photosynthesis and its importance to plant and animal life.

Curriculum Goals	Proficiency Objectives	Product	Additional Material
Plan investigations	Recognize parts of experiment	1. Score at least 80% on **test of vocabulary** from chapter. LS 1j 2. Demonstrate developing proficiency by identifying hypotheses, variables, and constants from sample experiments. LS 1f	Challenge 1: **Read** either Experiment 3 or Experiment 8 in *Experiments With Plants* by Salvatore Tocci, and pick one to do. Challenge 2: **Read** *Science Project Helper* by Mike Dickinson to develop new approaches to this exercise. LS 1f
Conduct investigations	Develop steps of experiment	1. List the major steps in this experiment and **define** each step. LS 1b, LS 4a 2. Describe how data will be collected and develop table for that purpose. LS 1 a, b, c, d	Challenge 1: Set up alternative part of experiment. Challenge 2: **Write** a description of how the class experiment could be developed into a science fair project. LS 1
Describe patterns in cell development	Visualize patterns	1. Draw a diagram of a plant cell identifying major organelles. LS 3a 2. **Describe** the function of organelles. LS 3b 3. Relate the connection between the source of nutrition and the development of cells. LS 3	Challenge 1: **Describe** the relationship between original exercise and the chosen one. Challenge 2: Develop one additional treatment for the plants and **predict** what will happen. LS 3b, LS 4a

Curriculum Goals	Proficiency Objectives	Product	Additional Material
Develop understanding of plant needs	Determining essential processes	1. Score at least 80% on a **test of basic plant functions**. LS 4a, LS 6a, b, c 2. Draw a diagram of the light phase and dark phase of cellular respiration. LS 6 a, b 3. **Write** a description of what happens in a cell when light energy is transformed into sugar. LS 6 a, b	Challenge 1: Either diagram what happened in the plants or write a description of what happened. LS 4, 6 Challenge 2: Make a poster of the one additional treatment to the plants. LS 1i, LS 4
Apply curricular theme	Plant needs for survival	1. In groups, **discuss** the effect of the various treatments on all of the plants. LS 4, LS 6 2. The groups will be divided into two groups and debate the effects of ground water pollution on plants. LS 1j, LS 3b	Challenge 1: **Evaluate** your experiment and the class version. LS 1i, j Challenge 2: **Discuss** how this experiment can be used as an example of the need for clean air and water. LS 4

SOURCE: Virginia Department of Education. (2005). *Life science standards of learning*. Retrieved July 26, 2005, from http://www.doe.virginia.gov/go/Sols/science7.pdf.

NOTE: Activities specifically targeted for girls are in **bold**.

135

Material," Challenge 1 refers to somewhat challenging material; it is appropriate for students who find the assigned work moderately easy and have finished the assigned material. Challenge 2 refers to very challenging material; it is appropriate for students who work well on their own and need further ideas to tackle.

You will notice that the products vary from reading, writing, and conducting experiments to working on the computer and working in groups. In a typical science classroom, each group of students (I usually use pairs) works together at one station on their experiment. The typical differentiated classroom has stations set up around the classroom that provide different activities, which must be completed for the students to finish the unit. In this unit, each group will have several plants to work with, as many plants as there are stations. At each station are directions for doing something different with a plant. Once all in the group have completed the basic requirements at a station, the group can move on to the next station.

Each student will have an individual plan of completion for the unit, and students involved in the additional challenges could be allowed to skip some of the basic product requirements if what they are doing covers the same material in a different way. A student who works slowly may be very good at drawing what the plants look like. That student may only meet the basic requirements for the reading section, but work on the highest challenge for the visual level.

The advantage of differentiating instruction is that each child can meet basic standards while the more capable children can be involved in activities that will stretch their abilities. In addition, children whose abilities vary across the curriculum will have the chance to excel in their strengths while they work on their academic weak points.

MULTIPLE INTELLIGENCES

In his theory of multiple intelligences, Howard Gardner (1983) proposed that, instead of being one concept, intelligence is composed of several different approaches to the world. He described different intelligences or ways that we can learn, and here we will use eight of the intelligences. Gardner's point is that intelligence involves far more than what has traditionally been the focus of education—reading, writing, and calculating. Teachers have found it very useful to think in terms of multiple intelligences when developing curricula or planning specific programs and have discovered that, using this theory, they can better meet the educational needs of all of their students (Lazear, 1992).

Even though most girls do well with verbally based instruction, not all do, and providing educational opportunities that use visual information and opportunities for manipulation will assure that all students' educational needs are met. Remember that girls tend to look at the big picture, and many of the activities in this sample unit require students to find specific information to substantiate their observations. This will help girls learn to produce evidence-based reports in science. Using multiple intelligences as a framework will help the teacher develop classroom exercises that reach a wide variety of student interests and abilities.

Tasks for Each of the Intelligences

The first three of Gardner's intelligences—verbal, logical, and visual—are related to conventional educational tasks and goals. What follows are lists of educational tasks directly related to each of the intelligences. You will find that some tasks appear on more than one list. For example, solving puzzles appears as an application for logical intelligence because the student must arrange the items in the puzzle in such a way that the answer can be revealed; solving puzzles also appears as an application for visual intelligence because the student may find the solution by looking at the various pieces to see where they fit together. When you find a task that appears on more than one list, you will generally discover that a larger proportion of your class will be engaged in the task.

Following are the eight intelligences with examples of academic applications.

- *Verbal*—reads, writes prose and poetry, discusses, listens, memorizes words, spells, builds vocabulary, speaks, debates, tells stories, communicates, plays word games
- *Logical*—calculates, solves problems, reasons, analyzes, experiments, organizes, determines relations, finds patterns and sequences, debates, uses symbols, plays chess and strategy games
- *Visual*—navigates, sees patterns, understands spatial relations, arranges, makes maps, charts, and graphs, builds models, draws, visualizes, solves puzzles, has good mechanical skills
- *Musical*—uses rhythms, recognizes and composes music, appreciates poetry, sings, whistles, keeps time, uses rhyme to learn, plays instruments, makes sound effects
- *Kinesthetic*—moves well, acts, plays sports, uses and understands body language with hand gestures, excels at hands-on learning, dances, does charades, can do sign language, experiments in lab, demonstrates coordination
- *Naturalistic*—grows plants, takes care of animals, observes nature, discovers patterns, classifies, sorts, determines similarities and differences, shows appreciation of environment, understands systems
- *Interpersonal*—works with others, has leadership skills, organizes and works in groups, makes friends, respects others, resolves conflicts, interviews, communicates
- *Intrapersonal*—understands self, is introspective and intuitive, sets realistic goals, understands own motivation, demonstrates planning and self-discipline, has clear values and strong will, is metacognitive

Most girls do well with applications from verbal, naturalistic, inter-personal, and intrapersonal intelligences. Many girls do not believe that they have strong logical skills, but it is my observation that, with practice, girls are very good at using logic to solve problems.

In Figure 7.2, you will find a unit using multiple intelligences in relation to the life science unit on the effect of various liquids on plants. Although each assignment specifies an activity for every intelligence, in practice, the teacher would pick several intelligences for each assignment, making sure that by the end of the unit all intelligences will be addressed.

LEARNING MODALITIES

You will remember that in Chapter 1 we examined how girls' sensory systems—hearing, vision, touch, smell, and taste—were different from those of boys and mentioned some ways that those differences can be used in the classroom. One paradigm used to frame instructional activities is that of learning modalities. In this instance, modality refers to the various sensory sources of information presented in class. Although smell and taste are certainly ways that we get information, the usual methods of receiving information in class are through our visual, auditory, and kinesthetic senses.

There are two types of visual information. One involves words, which require decoding—recognizing letters and being able to connect those letters into words that have meaning. The other involves icons—pictures, symbols, and representations that we recognize and can obtain meaning from. Therefore, the four learning modalities are visual-verbal, visual-iconic, auditory, and kinesthetic (Thies, 1999–2000). Here are some activities associated with each modality.

- *Visual-verbal*—reading, writing, journaling, developing vocabulary, and spelling
- *Visual-iconic*—using graphs and charts; highlighting; using symbols, pictures, and patterns
- *Auditory*—listening, singing, working in groups, giving a speech, and using rhyme
- *Kinesthetic*—doing hands-on activities, lab exercises, making models, and demonstrating

If you are not sure what learning modalities your students use, two versions of a short assessment are found in Chapter 8. One is for elementary-school teachers to fill out about their students, and the other is for middle- and high-school students to fill out on their own. A student has to have a certain amount of self-awareness before she can answer the questions accurately, and you will be the best judge of which instrument will work with your students. You may find some older elementary or younger

Figure 7.2   Multiple Intelligences Unit for Seventh-Grade Life Science

Purpose: To use basic principles to explore the effect of the environment on living organisms

Learning Standards (LS): Life Science, Grade 7 Standards of Learning addressed in this unit are the following:

LS 1: Conduct investigations

LS 3: Understand patterns of cellular organization

LS 4: Understand basic needs of organisms to carry out life processes

LS 6: Understand basic physical and chemical processes of photosynthesis

Learning Objectives: (1) Students will be able to plan and conduct investigations. (2) Students will investigate and understand that the basic needs of organisms must be met to carry out life processes. (3) Students will be able to investigate and understand the basic physical and chemical processes of photosynthesis and its importance to plant and animal life.

	Verbal	Logical	Visual	Musical	Kinesthetic	Naturalistic	Interpersonal	Intrapersonal
Skills	Reading, writing, listening	Calculating, problem solving, reasoning	Sense of direction, patterning	Recognition of music, use of rhythms	Physical activities, movement	Care of animals, categorizing, analyzing	Working with others, leadership	Understands self, knows direction of life
Assignment 1 Directions for Lab Week 1: Monday	**Read** the directions for the plant lab. LS 1	Plan the steps for carrying out the lab based on your hypothesis. LS 1	Draw a chart of what you are going to do in the lab. Take pictures of your plants. LS 1	**Research** the effect of music on plant development. LS 4	Design and set up the lab exercise. LS 1	Select what **plants** you will use in your lab. LS 3	**Develop questions** based on this material for the class. LS 1	What do you want to know about what is going to happen to the plants? **Write** your observations in a journal. LS 1

(Continued)

(Continued)

	Verbal	Logical	Visual	Musical	Kinesthetic	Naturalistic	Interpersonal	Intrapersonal
Assignment 2 **Read** Chapter 9, Section 1 Week 2: Monday	**Describe** the characteristics of seed plants. LS 3 a, b	Set up a chart to collect data from the lab exercise. LS 1 a, j	Draw pictures or diagrams of what has happened to the plants in one week. LS 4	Select two different types of music, put plants in different rooms with that music. LS 1	Start collecting the data on the plants using the chart you designed. LS 1	Look at what is happening to the other plants in the lab. Can you see any common events? LS 3, 4	**Get together** with everyone else whose plants are in the same conditions as yours. Compare notes. LS 4	**Make a journal entry** for today focusing on the differences in your plants in a week. LS 3
Assignment 3 **Read** Chapter 9, Section 2 Week 2: Tuesday	**Look up** the importance of gymnosperms in the past and in the present. LS 3, 6	Use your data chart to make a spreadsheet for your data. LS 1	Draw pictures of the cells that you see from your plants. LS 3	Check on the plants in the rooms with different music; **describe** the differences. LS 1	Refresh the liquid that your plants are growing in. LS 1	Take a portion of a leaf from each of your plants and look at it under the microscope. LS 3	**Talk** to someone who grows plants about their experiences. LS 6	**Make a journal entry** describing the differences in the cells in the plants. LS 3
Assignment 4 **Read** Chapter 9, Section 3 Week 2: Wednesday	**Compare and contrast** gymnosperms and angiosperms. LS 3, 6	Chart the similarities and differences between gymnosperms and angiosperms. LS 3	Draw pictures of both types of plants. LS 3	Look out of class for plants growing around music or noise. What do you see? LS 1	Make sure that your plants are receiving the correct treatment. LS 1g	Use samples of gymnosperms and angiosperms to show similarities and differences. LS 3	**Evaluate** the importance for humans of gymnosperms and angiosperms with the class. LS 4, 6	**Make a journal entry** describing how gymnosperms from the past are important to us now. LS 6

140

	Verbal	Logical	Visual	Musical	Kinesthetic	Naturalistic	Interpersonal	Intrapersonal
Assignment 5 **Read** Chapter 9 Section 4 Week 2: Thursday	**Describe** photosynthesis and its relationship to how plants grow. LS 4, 6	Finish collecting the data from your plants, making sure that you have correct units. LS 1	**Make a poster** of the light and dark cycles of photosynthesis. LS 6	**Memorize and recite a poem** about plants or flowers. LS 3	Crush a leaf from each plant with alcohol. Dip pieces of filter paper in each dish to see the different photochemicals. LS 6	Look at other plants at school or at home. Do you see any similarities to what is happening to the plants in the lab? LS 1	**Work in small groups** to answer questions about the importance of photosynthesis. LS 6	**Make a journal entry** reflecting on the importance of photosynthesis to humans. LS 4
Assignment 6 **Prepare for Quiz** Week 2: Friday	**Write** a report on this exercise. LS 1, 3, 4, 6	Use the spreadsheet to prepare a graph showing the changes in your plants over the two weeks. LS 1a	Take pictures of your plants at the end and compare them to ones from the beginning. Measure the differences. LS 1	Collect the plants growing in the noise/music rooms. **Compare** them to the other plants. LS 1, 6	Make a display of all of your data including your spreadsheet, photochemical strips, and descriptions. LS 6	**Research and describe** the effect of global warming on the two different types of plants. LS 4, 6	Debate the differences among the results from the different experiments, which helped the plants and which hurt the plants. LS 6	**Make a journal entry** for your observations on this lab exercise. LS 1, 3, 4, 6

SOURCE: Virginia Department of Education. (2005). *Life science standards of learning*. Retrieved July 26, 2005, from http://www.doe.virginia.gov/go/Sols/science7.pdf.

NOTE: Activities specifically targeted for girls are in **bold**.

middle-school students need your help filling out the form, but it can offer insights into how they learn best.

When using learning modalities to frame instructional activities, try to use at least three of the modalities in each lesson. It is easy to develop kinesthetic activities for subjects that involve hands-on learning, such as math and art, but it is much harder to develop verbal activities for these subjects. Conversely, language arts and history lend themselves to verbal activities, but developing hands-on activities may present a challenge.

Remember that girls develop verbal skills early, and they learn well from verbal stimuli, so their primary learning styles are usually visual-verbal and auditory (Honigsfeld & Dunn, 2003). Planning activities for either modality will help girls access the material. Additionally, most tests and assessments are primarily verbal, but lab exercises and math problems are usually visual-iconic and kinesthetic. Planning ways to give students a verbal way to report on lab exercises will help all students, as oral reports will benefit the auditory learner. You will find a sample science lesson plan for using learning modalities in Figure 7.3.

UNIT DESIGN

In their book *Understanding by Design* (2nd ed.), Wiggins and McTighe (2005) describe an approach to curriculum and assessment design that starts at the end and moves backward. The idea is that the best way to teach is first to decide what it is you want your students to know—what they should recognize, comprehend, and be familiar with. Once you have the end in mind, then you decide how you are going to determine or assess that your students have demonstrated that knowledge. It is important to consider a wide variety of assessment methods, including long- and short-term assessments, structured and fluid assessments, and evidence collected over time as well as that from a specific time, such as the end of a unit. Finally, instruction can be framed so that the students gain the knowledge and information the teacher believes is important to know.

An obvious complaint about this method of design is that it emphasizes assessments and pays less attention to the process of learning. In fact, the focus is on what students are to come away with from the learning experience, not on their grade in the class. This design actually encourages teachers to develop a wide variety of approaches and to utilize different techniques to ensure that all students have the chance to learn.

In addition to turning the process of curriculum design on its head, the principles of backward design also involve several steps that help the teacher rethink the planning process and result in a more comprehensive curriculum. Following an identification of the state standards, which will be addressed by the unit, Wiggins and McTighe (2005) present six ways to identify when students have developed true knowledge.

Figure 7.3 Learning Styles Unit for Seventh-Grade Life Science

Purpose: To use basic principles to explore the effect of the environment on living organisms

Learning Standards (LS): Life Science, Grade 7 Standards of Learning addressed in this unit are the following:

  LS 1: Conduct investigations

  LS 3: Understand patterns of cellular organization

  LS 4: Understand basic needs of organisms to carry out life processes

  LS 6: Understand basic physical and chemical processes of photosynthesis

Learning Objectives: (1) Students will be able to plan and conduct investigations. (2) Students will investigate and understand that the basic needs of organisms must be met to carry out life processes. (3) Students will be able to investigate and understand the basic physical and chemical processes of photosynthesis and its importance to plant and animal life.

Assignment	Visual-Verbal	Visual-Iconic	Auditory	Kinesthetic
1. Directions for Lab Week 1: Monday	**Read** directions for lab exercise. **Formulate a hypothesis** about what you think is going to happen in your lab journal. LS 1	Draw a chart of what you are going to do in the lab. Take pictures of your plants. LS 1	**Collaborate** with your lab partner to decide what you are going to do in the lab. **Compare** observations. LS 1	Select what plants you will use in your lab and set up the lab exercise. LS 1
2. **Read** Chapter 9, Section 1 Week 2: Monday	**Describe** the characteristics of seed plants. **Make a journal entry** for today focusing on the differences in your plants in a week. LS 3 a, b	Set up a chart to collect data from the lab exercise. Draw pictures or diagrams of what has happened to the plants in one week. LS 1 a, j, LS 4	**Listen** to the teacher lecture on the basics of plants. **Take notes** on that lecture. LS 3	Organize the data you collect by entering the information on the plants using the chart you designed. LS 1

(Continued)

Assignment	Visual-Verbal	Visual-Iconic	Auditory	Kinesthetic
3. **Read** Chapter 9, Section 2 Week 2: Tuesday	**Look up** the importance of gymnosperms in the past and in the present. **Make a journal entry** describing the differences in the cells in the plants. LS 3, 6	Use your data chart to make a spreadsheet for your data. Draw pictures of the cells that you see from your plants. LS 1, 3	**Discuss** the progress of the plants with others in the class. LS 1	Refresh the liquid that your plants are growing in. Take a portion of a leaf from each of your plants and look at it under the microscope. LS 1, 3
4. **Read** Chapter 9, Section 3 Week 2: Wednesday	**Compare and contrast** gymnosperms and angiosperms. **Make a journal entry** describing how gymnosperms from the past are important to us now. LS 3, 6	Draw pictures of both types of plants. **Make a chart** of the similarities and differences between gymnosperms and angiosperms. LS 3	**Discuss** the differences between gymnosperms and angiosperms with the class. LS 4, 6	Make sure that your plants are receiving the correct treatment. Predict what will happen to them by the end of the experiment. LS 1g
5. **Read** Chapter 9 Section 4 Week 2: Thursday	**Describe** photosynthesis and its relationship to how plants grow. **Make a journal entry** describing why photosynthesis is so important to humans. LS 4, 6	**Make a poster** of the light and dark cycles of photosynthesis. LS 6	**Memorize and recite** a poem about plants or flowers. **Work in small groups** to answer questions on the importance of photosynthesis. LS 3, 6	Crush a leaf from each plant with alcohol. Dip strips of filter paper in each dish and see what different photochemicals are released. LS 6
6. **Prepare for Quiz,** Week 2: Friday	**Write** a report on this exercise or **make a journal entry** on your results. LS 1, 3, 4, 6	Use the spreadsheet to prepare a graph showing the changes in your plants over the two weeks. LS 1 a, e	Debate the differences among the results from the different experiments, which helped the plants and which hurt the plants. LS 6	Make a display of all of your data including your spreadsheet, your photochemical strips, pictures of your plants, and your descriptions. LS 6

SOURCE: Virginia Department of Education. (2005). *Life science standards of learning.* Retrieved July 26, 2005, from http://www.doe.virginia.gov/go/Sols/science7.pdf.

NOTE: Activities specifically targeted for girls are in **bold**.

- *Explanation*—can the student give details and describe events, fact, and data?
- *Interpretation*—can the student relate the information to other situations, give metaphors, or provide examples?
- *Application*—can the student translate the information to novel situations, adapting the principles to the new context?
- *Perspective*—can the student see the information from the point of view of another?
- *Empathy*—can the student understand how another feels or perceives the information?
- *Self-Knowledge*—can the student understand what she does not do well and what is easy for her to understand based on her own perspective and learning style?

The third step, in which the teacher plans activities and learning opportunities to ensure that the students can understand the information, is based on what Wiggins and McTighe (2005) call the WHERETO design principles:

Where are we headed?—this is a preassessment to find out what information students have and what they want to learn about the subject.

Hook and hold—this is the presentation of information designed to increase the interest of the students about the information.

Explore and experience, enable and equip—this is work designed to assist the student build understanding about the subject.

Reflect, rethink, revise—this asks the student to review the information and reassess what she knows.

Evaluate work and progress—this is the presentation of final projects, tests, or other means that the teacher has identified at the beginning of the process to indicate that the student has reached full understanding.

Tailor and personalize the work—this is attention to each individual student's learning requirements and differentiating instruction.

Organize for optimal effectiveness—without this step, there is no way to ensure that the lesson accomplishes its goals (Wiggins & McTighe, 2005).

You will find a lesson plan for your hypothetical science class using unit design in Figure 7.4.

146

Figure 7.4 Example of Unit Design

SEVENTH-GRADE LIFE SCIENCE

Virginia Standard

Learning Standard (LS) 1: The student will plan and conduct investigations in which

a. data are organized into tables showing repeated trials and means

b. variables are defined

c. metric units (International System of Units [SI]) are used

d. sources of experimental error are defined

e. dependent variables, independent variables, and constants are identified

f. variables are controlled to test hypotheses, and trials are repeated

i. interpretations from a set of data are evaluated and defended

j. an understanding of the nature of science is developed and reinforced

LS 3: The student will investigate and understand that all living things show patterns of cellular organization. Key concepts include the following:

a. cells, tissues, organs, and systems

b. life functions and processes of cells, tissues, organs, and systems (respiration, removal of wastes, growth, reproduction, digestion, and cellular transport)

LS 4: The student will investigate and understand that the basic needs of organisms must be met to carry out life processes. The key concept is the following:

a. plant needs (light, water, gases, and nutrients)

LS 6: The student will investigate and understand the basic physical and chemical processes of photosynthesis and its importance to plant and animal life. Key concepts include

a. energy transfer between sunlight and chlorophyll

b. transformation of water and carbon dioxide into sugar and oxygen

c. photosynthesis as the foundation of virtually all food webs

Enduring Understandings or Unit Learning Objectives

1. Student will be able to (SWBAT) communicate ideas and information orally in an organized and succinct manner.

2. SWBAT identify all parts of an experimental investigation, collect data, and evaluate the results.

3. SWBAT correctly name all parts of a plant and a plant cell and show what life functions involve each part of the plant or cell.

4. SWBAT describe the process of plant growth, photosynthesis, and the effect of pollution on plants.

5. SWBAT draw conclusions about the effect of environments on plants based on explicit and implied information.

6. SWBAT elaborate the connection between plants and the world food web.

Facets of Understanding

Explanation: SWBAT identify accurately the main parts of a plant and plant cell.

Interpretation: SWBAT examine the progress of the plants in the lab exercise and be able to explain the process.

Application: SWBAT explain how the information gained in this lab will relate to growing plants on a large scale.

Perspective: SWBAT identify the views of farmers on the environment and of manufacturers to do business with limited effect on the environment.

Empathy: SWBAT openly discuss different opinions of manufacturers and environmentalists.

Self-Knowledge: SWBAT will demonstrate an understanding of personal beliefs about various environmental pressures on plants.

(Continued)

147

Figure 7.4 (Continued)

		DETERMINE ACCEPTABLE EVIDENCE			
National or State Standard	Learning Objective or Essential Understanding for the Unit	Learning Experiences (Assignments, Instruction)	Assessment Methods (Evidence and Should Include Self-assessment)	Performance Criteria or Grading Standards	Accommodations or Modifications for Gender Differences
LS 1: The student will plan and conduct investigations in which a. data are organized into tables showing repeated trials and means b. variables are defined c. metric units (SI-International System of Units) are used e. sources of experimental error are defined	1. SWBAT develop a hypothesis, and design an experiment to test that hypothesis with variables, controls, and constants. 2. SWBAT develop a data collection plan which provides for proper scientific units. 3. SWBAT conduct experiment, collect data, and describe events.	Reading assignments in text followed by classroom discussion. View video on environmental effects on plants and discuss options for solutions to problems. Students will identify the key functions in the life processes of plants and be able to explain what happens and why it is important.	Unit test with various types of questions. ***Product:*** Solutions to problem of pollution for plants ***Product:*** Identification of crucial steps in photosynthesis and how that is the basis for all food on earth ***Product:*** Student group work ***Product:*** Science bee score	Test will be 15% of unit grade. Homework completion will be 15% of grade. Lab report will be 20% of grade. Half of the grade will be based on a written account of the lab exercise and half of the grade on the accompanying data analysis. An additional 5% will be given for responsibility in managing the lab. Participation in the class discussion about what pollution means and its effect on plants and humans will be 15%.	Movement of students in class will be encouraged and teacher will create different locations in room where students can work in groups. Competition among the students will be used to check knowledge of facts. Begin each unit with a discussion about the general concepts that will be covered and what the outcomes will be. Focus on how the students can relate to the effect of pollution on society.

National or State Standard	Learning Objective or Essential Understanding for the Unit	Learning Experiences (Assignments, Instruction)	Assessment Methods (Evidence and Should Include Self-assessment)	Performance Criteria or Grading Standards	Accommodations or Modifications for Gender Differences
f. dependent variables, independent variables, and constants are identified g. variables are controlled to test hypotheses, and trials are repeated i. interpretations from a set of data are evaluated and defended j. an understanding of the nature of science is developed and reinforced	4. SWBAT interpret the data and relate the events to the larger world seeing how science explains environmental events.	Students will be divided into groups and each group will be assigned a different part of a plant cell. They will research that part of the cell and then either get together to discuss how the parts of the cell work together or become the cell by working together to see how the parts work together. Use different sized balls for various molecules such as sugar, water, and nitrogen so that the "organelles" can do their work.		Either writing a narrative showing how plants are affected at the cellular level by pollution or making a chart of that relationship will be 20%. Score on Science Bee will be 10%.	Encourage collaborative work with small groups of students working together.

(Continued)

Figure 7.4 (Continued)

WHERETO FOR GIRLS

(Teacher Considerations and Questions to Address)

Where Are You Headed?	Hook Your Students	Experiences	Reflect and Rethink	Evaluation	Tailor	Organize
Introductory Discussion: Have students collaborate for a few minutes on what they know about plants and the effect of environmental damage on plants. Each group will put three points on the board from the list that they develop in their groups. **Performance Criteria:** *Content:* Describe accurately the major events in the life processes of plants. **Process:** Collaborate on research project on the effect of various common liquids on plants. **Quality:** Detailed information on the investigation is required. Presentations must be completed and include both a written report and a visual presentation of the data.	**Hooks:** Bring flowers into the classroom and give them to the girls to look at. Bring in carnations colored by drawing up colored water into their petals. Take girls to a botanical garden for a tour by a horticulturist or have a gardener visit the classroom.	Reading assignments in text followed by classroom discussion. Students will view video on environmental effects on plants and discuss options for solutions to problems. Students will identify the key functions in the life processes of plants and be able to explain what happens and why it is important. Students will be divided into groups and each group will be assigned a different part of a plant cell. They will research that part of the cell and then get together to discuss how the parts of the cell work together.	**Prompts:** Thought questions describing the change in plants over time as the various solutions are drawn up into the plants. Discuss what pollution means and its effect on plants and humans. Write a narrative showing how plants are affected at the cellular level by pollution.	Unit test with various types of questions. **Product:** Solutions to problem of pollution for plants **Product:** Identification of crucial steps in photosynthesis and how that is the basis for all food on earth **Product:** Student group work **Product:** Science bee score	**Differentiation Strategies:** Make sure that groups of girls are in twos or fours, not threes. Divide students into two groups for a science bee. The teams will compete on knowledge of the subject, and each team will confer before answering so that all students in the team agree with the answer.	**Revisions/ Rehearsals:** Peer review of timelines to check for accuracy. Check calendar every other day to keep students on track to meet deadlines. Students will submit rough drafts of the document accompanying the map.

150

WHERETO FOR BOYS

(Teacher Considerations and Questions to Address)

Where Are You Headed?	Hook Your Students	Experiences	Reflect and Rethink	Evaluation	Tailor	Organize
Introductory Discussion: Have boys make a chart of all of the various environmental factors that impact the success of plants. Make a mind web showing how all of those factors are interrelated. **Performance Criteria:** *Content:* Describe accurately the major events in the life processes of plants. **Process:** Collaborate on research project on the effect of various common liquids on plants. **Quality:** Detailed information on the investigation is required. Presentations must be completed and include both a written report and a visual presentation of the data.	**Hooks:** Have the boys use the Internet to discover all of the pollutants that result from the automobile industry. Give the boys various solutions to spray on flowers to see what the immediate effect is. Solutions could be hot water, ice water, hair spray, mild bleach solution, vinegar solution, hydrogen peroxide, and the like.	Reading assignments in text followed by classroom discussion. Students will view video on environmental effects on plants and discuss options for solutions to problems. Students will identify the key functions in the life processes of plants and be able to explain what happens and why it is important. Students will be divided into groups and each group will be assigned a different part of a plant cell. They will research that part of the cell and then become the cell by working together to see how the parts work together. Use different size balls for various molecules, such as sugar, water, and nitrogen so that the "organelles" can do their work.	**Prompts:** Thought questions describing the change in plants over time as the various solutions are drawn up into the plants. Boys may make charts showing how the solutions affect the plants. Discuss what pollution means and its effect on plants and humans. Relate the pollutants from the automobile industry to the effects on plants in their immediate vicinity.	Unit test with various types of questions. **Product:** Solutions to problem of pollution for plants **Product:** Identification of crucial steps in photosynthesis and how that is the basis for all food on earth **Product:** Student group work **Product:** Science bee score	**Differentiation Strategies:** When boys are working on their projects, allow them to find their own space to work together, and that may mean sitting or lying on the floor. Divide students into two groups for a science bee. The teams will have three members and will compete on knowledge of the subject for prizes (e.g., stickers, a free homework pass).	**Revisions/ Rehearsals:** Peer review of timelines to check for accuracy. Check calendar every other day to keep students on track to meet deadlines. Students will submit rough drafts of the document.

SOURCE: Wiggins, G., & McTighe, J. (2005). *Understanding by design* (2nd ed.). Alexandria, VA: Association for Supervision and Curriculum Development.

EMPOWERING GIRLS AS LEARNERS

The purpose of this book is to provide teachers with ideas, options, and techniques that will make their classrooms more welcoming to all kinds of learners. We all know that by enlarging our repertoire of methods and approaches we can do a better job in our classrooms. The best part is that we will help all of our students, not just the girls who may be having trouble in some areas.

The real challenge is to help all students become autonomous learners. Most girls do well in school so that when they have trouble they take it personally and see their shortcomings as personal failures. You can make a real difference in the life of your students if you can get them to understand that their difficulties are probably not due to an inability to learn certain material, but to a failure of an approach to learning. Changing the method they use to learn the subject can make a world of difference. I have successfully taught "box the operator" to many girls who were convinced they could not do word problems only to find that if they changed their approach they could solve even complicated problems. It is confidence that makes the difference for girls and when they are sure they have a solution path, they do well.

TEST-TAKING STRATEGIES

Although we make every effort to give our students a variety of ways to demonstrate what they have learned, national standardized tests and other landmark tests continue to benefit verbal learners. For some girls this is an advantage, but for others, test anxiety and poor test-taking strategies mean that their poor test-taking skills present hurdles they find almost impossible to overcome.

Girls may suffer from test anxiety and we covered methods to help your students deal with that in Chapter 3. All forms of anxiety are helped when the sufferer is prepared and believes that she has some skills she can use in the relevant situation. Remember, if the anxiety is severe—the student gets noticeably pale, sweats, trembles, cries, becomes belligerent—before or during a test, refer the student to your school counselor for assistance. On the other hand, acquiring test-taking strategies has helped many students become more confident in their abilities resulting in reduced test anxiety.

Beginning Strategies

Step 1

Determine what types of questions are easier and what are harder for the student. The easiest way to do this is to sit down with the student and several of her tests. Look at the items she has the most trouble and the least trouble answering.

Ask her the following:

- Why does she think she has trouble with certain types of items and finds others easier?
- How did she study for the test?
- What kinds of questions did she study for?
- How does she go about answering the questions?
- What did she think the question was asking?

If the problem is lack of study strategies or test preparation, help students acquire better study strategies. The learning style assessment in Chapter 8 will help you and the student discover how the student prefers to learn. For example, a student who prefers to learn through an auditory modality can study by reciting the material out loud or she can record the material and play it back to herself.

Step 2

If the student's problem is that she does not understand what response the question is asking for—a common difficulty—there are several steps that will help.

a. Have the student read the question out loud to you and ask her what the answer should look like. Some students are not aware that essay questions require complete sentences or that questions asking for an outline do not.
b. Make sure that the student understands what is meant by terms such as discuss, describe, compare and contrast, diagram, outline, define, list, summarize, and so forth.
c. Have the student prepare questions for the material. When students do this, they frequently find that they understand what other questions are asking for.
d. During a test, when the student gets to the type of item with which she has difficulty, have her come to your desk or step outside with you and talk over strategies for answering the item. You don't want to know what she is going to put in her answer, but how she is going to organize her answer.

Step 3

Adapt study techniques to the type of test anticipated. Studying material in the same way that you will be asked to recall it uses what psychologists call *context-dependent memory*. For example, families frequently help children prepare for a spelling test by calling out words and having the child spell the word out loud. However, if the test is written, the poor speller may have trouble writing down the correct spelling she has practiced by saying the spelling. If the test is to be written, the better technique is for someone to call out the words and have the child write the correct spelling. If the child is preparing for a spelling bee, then the child should spell the words out loud. Copying notes is an old technique that works well for some students, as does taking notes from notes—called *squeeze notes*. The advantage is that when the student gets to the test, she has a memory of having written the material several times before. Writing material over and over improves memory (Naka, 1998).

Step 4

Encourage study groups. Girls will get together to study and, if that is what they do, they will benefit from the collaboration. The problem is that the study session may turn into a chat session and little studying gets done. I always recommended to my students that they plan for some chitchat by structuring their time. It will help if they have a study agenda or study plan that is not too ambitious, fits the time available, and gives them a set amount of time for general conversation. If they don't do this from the beginning, girls may never get around to the academic work they set out to cover.

Strategies for Specific Item Types

The first step is to read the directions—this is the most underutilized hint. Directions may help provide clues to answering the questions. Frequently, tests ask the student to answer three of five questions, or the like, and answering all of them will take up time, at the very least. Girls may read the directions and then answer all of the parts because they want to make sure that they have three correct out of the five given. I solve this by grading the first three answers that are given. I tell the students that I am neither a mind reader nor a fortune-teller and it is not my job to guess which ones they want to use or select the answers most likely to be correct. Part of the question is finding out what the student is sure she knows.

Objective Questions

These present difficulties for many girls because, as we mentioned earlier, the answer is the answer; there is no room for mistakes. Consequently, some girls are threatened by these items, which they see as designed to catch them in small mistakes. They see essay or free response questions as easier, as they allow them to write enough down so that they are sure they have produced enough information to contain the answer.

Giving girls these strategies helps. One of my students was missing almost all of the multiple-choice items on the science test and dragging her overall grade to a low C. After she and I covered the following suggestions, her grades improved to high B's and even A's simply because she was not second-guessing herself.

- Answer objective questions first. Information that will help answer other questions may be found in objective questions. Another advantage is the principle of priming. Simply seeing words and concepts contained in the objective questions reminds a student of basic concepts, which may help her remember more material.
- For true/false questions, look for criterion words such as never, always, most, least, some, frequently, rarely, and the like. The more extreme the criterion, the less likely the statement is to be true, and the more ambiguous the criterion, the more likely the statement is to be true.
- For matching questions, read the right-hand list first, then the left-hand list all the way through. The student should match the choices she is sure of first and cross out the items in the right-hand list that have been used. Then compare the remaining terms and definers to solve the rest of the problem by eliminating choices known to be incorrect. Do not let the students draw lines from terms to definers, as the resulting web will be hard to interpret.
- For multiple-choice questions, direct students to cover the choices, read the question, and try to provide an answer for the question. Then have them look at the choices. If their answer is there, they know they are correct and can move on. If their answer is not there, have them look at the choices and see if they can immediately see the answer. If they cannot, direct them to move on and leave the question for the moment. When they have finished the section, they should go back and go through the same process again. Their brains will have been thinking about the question even if they are not aware of it and the answer will frequently jump out at them. Multiple-choice items can be the most difficult for some girls, as they try to make all the answers fit. Some of my students have frozen when they are faced with three correct choices and are asked to pick the best one. These suggestions are not foolproof, but they can help students break out of an impasse.
  - Read the question carefully to see if more than one answer can be correct. In which case, all of the above may be the correct answer.
  - Which choice is the most inclusive? That is, are any of the choices part of another choice? The one that contains the other may be the correct choice. For example, if four choices are—monocot plants, flower parts in threes, parallel veins on leaves, and vascular bundles scattered in the stem, monocot plants is the answer because it describes the other three.

- o Are some of the choices similar or tending in the same direction? For example, if four choices are up, down, ascending, rising, down is likely to be the answer because it is in a different direction.
- o There is some thought that the longest answer is correct because it contains the most information. That can be true; however, if the answer contains a lot of complicated language, it may simply be a decoy.
- o Only change answers if you are totally sure the first answer is incorrect. Research shows that frequently answers that were changed were correct to begin with.
- o Dealing with reverse questions, such as ones that ask for the one answer that is not correct, can be difficult. Answer the question in the positive and look for the one answer that is not correct; that will be the answer to the negative question. For example, a question asks which of the following *are not* ducks, and the choices are teal, mallard, wood, and swan. Ask yourself, which of the following *are* ducks. Your answer will be teal, mallard, and wood. Swans are not ducks so they are the answer to the negative question.
- o Work backward: Eliminate the wrong answers until you find the right one. If you can't decide between two, guess as you have a 50–50 chance of being correct.
- • For completion questions, direct students to read the sentence carefully to see if they know the answer or if they can determine the answer from cues in the sentence. Pay particular attention to grammar, as this will give hints. Check to see if the word or phrase to be supplied starts with a consonant or a vowel (the blank is preceded by *a* or *an*) or if the word is to be plural. If the student is still not sure of the answer, she should leave the question and come back to it later—she may be surprised to find that she can then supply the answer. The reason is that by taking the test, she is reading and thinking about the material, which may provide some cue to remembering the answer.

Essay or Free-Response Questions

Girls may believe that essay questions are easy as they can use their verbal fluency to produce many words to answer these questions. However, the problem for some girls is that a lack of focus and coherence means that their answers simply provide disconnected thoughts. In teaching girls how to answer essay questions effectively, have them outline answers first before beginning to write. They will find that the time is well spent, as their answers will be more coherent and cohesive.

- Read all parts of the question first. The question may be structured in such a way as to create a framework for the answer. Some questions are asked so that there is a logical progression of the information. This is a design to assist the student who may have trouble with the material. I have had students look at the first part, answer the whole question and then reply "see answer to first part" for all of the remaining sections.

- Decide what kind of answer is required. This will be determined by what the question asks for, such as to discuss, describe, analyze, justify, and the like. If the question asks the student to compare and contrast, the student may list the information from each part and then indicate the sections that the parts have in common by drawing lines between them or underlining them. If the student prefers to use a Venn diagram, she can put the information that is shared in the intersection of the circles and information that is unique to each topic inside the circles, but outside of the intersection. Either way, the student then has all the information already organized to write the essay. If the student gets stuck or paralyzed by all the possibilities for answers, have her outline the answer, as that will keep her on task and let the teacher know that the student really did know some of the information.

- Restate the question in the first sentence. This helps provide structure, gives the student a place to start, and lets the teacher know that the student is answering the right question.

- Be careful not to use circular reasoning. That happens when a term is used to identify itself and does not indicate that the student knows what the term means. I frequently ask my psychology students to define random selection, and many will answer something like, "Random selection occurs when subjects are randomly selected to participate in a study." The student does not actually have to know what either random or selection means to provide that answer.

- Help students learn to "read" the teacher. Point out parts of the material that you have stressed and help them understand that the test will focus on that material. Girls have an advantage in their ability to use subtle cues to read people, but they don't always focus on the right material. However, many girls can easily learn this skill.

FINAL WORDS

What I hope to accomplish with this book is to alert teachers to the fact that girls and boys do not think and reason in the same ways, and that affects what happens in your classroom. Just because a girl is not doing well in your classroom, do not assume that she cannot learn the material. Look carefully at what she is doing. See if you can help her understand where her problem lies with the material, and help her develop alternative approaches to the lessons.

Girls need your support, as there is so much in their lives that works against them to succeed academically especially in the science, technology, engineering, and math (STEM) courses. They may not ever want to continue in these courses into college, but they should be given the chance to do well. The problem in the past was that society assumed that girls would not be capable in math and science and never offered opportunities. Girls can do well in math and science and many enjoy the subjects. Help those girls find the spark that may light their way to a career. Your students are lucky to have you as their teacher.

8

Resources
and Other Help

In previous chapters, I have mentioned that you would find some resources at the end of the book. This is the place. The items here are not in any particular order, but they will give you some information or tools to help you with your students.

MATH TECHNIQUES

The following two sections are techniques for teaching math to girls. Although it may seem odd to remind math teachers to say everything, I have frequently noticed that many math teachers either assume that students understand the basic steps or are so used to doing math silently for themselves that they forget to verbalize what they are doing. I will reiterate my belief that this may be the single most effective practice that exists to help students who have trouble with math. The reason is that if a student is a verbal-auditory learner, seeing someone solve problems provides no useful information. These students need to either read a description of what to do or need to hear someone tell them what to do. Also, the verbal learner may have difficulties recognizing icons, so every time a teacher presents a symbol whether it is a sign indicating that the problem requires dividing ($\div$) or a letter representing an element (K for potassium), the teacher needs to provide the words that are associated with those symbols.

Verbalizing Math

Frequently, the teacher puts a problem on the board without saying what is being written. Then the teacher will say something like, "Then, what you do is this . . ." and simply perform each step visually without saying it. Try the following approach instead (what the teacher says is in "quotes," and what is written on the board is in **bold**).

1. "The next problem is two x plus four x equals twelve" (while you are writing **2x + 4x = 12** on the board).

2. "What is the first step to solve this problem?" A student will answer that you should combine like terms. "Exactly, combine like terms. Can you identify the like terms for the class?" The student will point out that the terms that share an x are the like terms. *"What do you mean by combine?"* A student should tell you that means add. "Correct. That means that we will add the x terms. Tell the class, please, what I should write down." The student should tell you that two x plus four x adds up to six x. Put that on the board **(2x + 4x = 6x).** "What do I do with the right-hand side of the equation?" A student should tell you that it does not change, and you bring down the equals sign and the number on the right side of the equation (while you write **6x = 12** on the board).

3. "Now what do we do?" A student will answer that you should divide both sides by six. "Very good, divide both sides by the same number. How do we write that so everyone can see how we do that?" A student should answer that you draw a line under each number and put a six under the line. "So I'm going to draw a line under both terms and put a six below. Why does that mean that I'm dividing by six?" (You write $\frac{6x}{6} = \frac{12}{6}$ on the next line). A student will say that the line indicates division. "Correct. Remember, you can do that as long as you perform the same operation on both sides of the equation."

4. "So now, if I divide six into six here on the left, what do I write down?" (**Cross out both sixes** on the left.) A student will respond with one. "Perfect, one it is" (and you write **1** next to the crossed out sixes).

5. "If I divide six into twelve here on the right, what do I write down?" (**Cross out the 6 and the 12.**) A student will respond with two. "You got it" (put a **2** next to the term on the right).

6. "So, what terms are left for me to write down for the last step?" A student should respond with x equals two (and you write **x = 2).**

This takes much longer to write than it does to say, and as you get used to saying every step out loud, you will get better at it. Also, this is the way I teach students to solve simple equations, and your method may be different. The point is to say everything that you are doing, whatever method you use. Teachers who are working with problems such as the one used in this example may be surprised that these directions are here, as generally teachers at this level do just what is suggested. It is teachers of higher-level math and above who forget to say everything.

Box the Operator

This process was taught to me many years ago, and I find that it works well for students in upper-elementary math and in pre-algebra. Once you are familiar with the principles, this works very well to help students figure out how to solve word problems at any level.

Figure 8.1   Box the Operator

If the problem is

- If three times a number is increased by seven, the result is the same as when 72 is decreased by twice the number.

1. The first step is to *box the operator*. Before the advent of highlighters, we drew a box around all of the words that stand for mathematical operations. Now, however, the box can be indicated by a highlighter, usually yellow. So, once that is done, the problem looks like this:

   - If three **times** a number is **increased** by seven, the result is the same as when 72 is **decreased** by tw**ice** the number.

   You will note that twice is only half highlighted because it is both a number and an operation.

2. The second step is to underline all of the numbers—I use a red pen to do this to make the numbers stand out. Once that is done, the problem looks like this:

   - If three **times** a number is **increased** by seven, the result is the same as when 72 is **decreased** by twice the number.

   You will note that only half of *twice* is underlined, to indicate that it also represents a number.

3. The third step is to find the equals sign, after all, this is an equation. I use a green highlighter, but without color here, I have indicated it with a pair of arrows so the problem will look like this:

   - If three **times** a number is **increased** by seven, the result is the same as when 72 is **decreased** by twice the number.

4. The fourth step is to mark the variables or, if you prefer, what is unknown. Here it is important for the student to decide if the variables are the same or if they are different. In this problem, the "number" is the same in both places, so it can be given the same mark, such as a circle around them. With circles, the problem now looks like this:

   - If three **times** a number is **increased** by seven, the result is the same as when 72 is **decreased** by twice the number.

(Continued)

(Continued)

In two variable equations, there must be different ways to mark the separate variables. The easiest way is to circle the variables with different colored pens or pencils. The shape of the mark will indicate that what is marked is a variable and the difference will indicate that the variables are not the same.

5. The last step is simply to write the problem as it is marked:

3 times number increased 7 = 72 decreased 2 times number

Then, turn the words into symbols and the word problem now looks like this:

$3 \times N + 7 = 72 - 2 \times N$

The same process can be used to dissemble a word problem. Remember that operators are shaded, numbers are underlined, variables are circled, and the equals sign is marked with arrows or a different highlighter.
So this is how a word problem would be marked:

A farmer, who grows cabbages, harvests 800 cabbages to send to market. He sent them to three different markets. He sent 270 to the first market, and he sent 150 more cabbages to the second market than to the third market. How many cabbages did he send to the second market?

$800 = 270 + 150 + C + C$

BOOKS

What follows is a list of books or references that you might find useful. The list is in alphabetic order and is not listed in any order of significance.

This list is, certainly, not exhaustive. They are simply books that friends of mine or I have used and found to be helpful.

Books With Interesting and Simple Science Experiments

Hanauer, E. (1968). *Biology experiments for children.* New York: Dover.
Mandell, M. (1968). *Physics experiments for children.* New York: Dover.
Mebane, R. C., & Rybolt, T. R. *Adventures with atoms and molecules: Chemistry experiments for young people.* Hillside, NJ: Enslow.

There are four different books in this Mebane and Rybolt work. I have the original hardback set published from 1985–1992. Paperback versions published in 1998 are also available. These are true *kitchen-sink experiments.* That means they can be done with commonly available substances and equipment and are generally perfectly safe for even the youngest of students.

Norris, J., & Davis, C. (2000). *Science experiments for young learners.* Monterey: Evan-Moor.
Mullin, V. L. (1968). *Chemistry experiments for children.* New York: Dover.
Reuben, G. (1968). *Electricity experiments for children.* New York: Dover.
Tocci, S. (2001). *True books: Science experiments.* Connecticut: Children's Press.

Titles in this series include *Experiments with rocks and minerals. Experiments with solids, liquids, and gases. Experiments with energy. Experiments with simple machines. Experiments with magnets. Experiments with soap. Experiments with plants. Experiments with motion. Experiments with electricity. Experiments with foods. Experiments with water. Experiments with air, copper, oxygen, hydrogen, and the noble gases. Gold. Nitrogen. Carbon. The periodic table.*

VanCleave, J. (1990). *Science for every kid.* Jossey-Bass.

Titles in this series include *Biology, Earth Science, Chemistry, Physics, The Human Body, Food and Nutrition, Engineering, Oceans, Astronomy, Constellations, Ecology, Geography,* and *Machines.*

Books With Interesting Approaches to Math

Note: All can be found at MindWare (www.MindWareonline.com).

Addition Adventures, Subtraction Secrets, Multiplication Mosaics, More Multiplication Mosaics, Division Designs, Decimal Destinations, and Fraction Finders. This series gives math drill and the answers, solves problems, gives answers, or creates designs.

Logic Links and *Noodlers* (also *Noodlers Puzzle Box*)—workbooks using color and shapes to teach logic and spatial relationships.

Math Challenge—ages 8–10—creative word problems that are based on everyday situations.

Math Minutes—Grades 1–8 and middle school versions. Designed to increase math fluency.

Math Perplexors—Level A (ages 8–9), Level B (ages 9–10), Level C (ages 10–11) Level D (ages 12 and up)—these workbooks provide story problems that require logic to solve.

Modern Patterns Coloring Book—practice with patterns for spatial skills.

Sequencers (ages 8–10)—workbook with exercises similar to Mastermind.

Rappaport, J. (1999). *Algebra survival guide: A conversational guide for the thoroughly befuddled* and *Algebra survival workbook.* Santa Fe, NM: Singing Turtle Press. (These can be found from any book supplier.)

WEB SITES

In an attempt to interest girls in science and math, various individuals and organizations have posted information on the Web. I am sure I have missed some important ones, and if you know of any, please let me know so that these lists can be more complete.

Engineering Web Sites for Girls

These are groups dedicated to increasing the visibility of engineering as a career for women and providing mentors for women who are considering entering this field.

The Extraordinary Women Engineers project of the American Society of Civil Engineers. http://www.engineeringwomen.org/

The Institute of Electrical and Electronics Engineers (IEEE) Women in Engineering (WIE) project. http://www.ieee.org/portal/pages/committee/women/index.html
    The National Academy of Engineering sponsored site, Engineer Girl! http://www.engineergirl.org/

The Society of Women Engineers. http://www.swe.org/

Science Program Web Sites for Girls

This list is not exhaustive, but simply some of the better-known programs. Most universities are sponsoring girls' science programs and certainly can assist you in finding individuals who will help you develop programs for your students.

A list of math and science summer camps for girls can be found at http://www.education-world.com/a_curr/curr238.shtml

DragonflyTV SciGirls is a program sponsored by Public Television, and although the camps and programs are not numerous at the moment, the program is growing. There may be one near you. http://pbskids.org/dragonflytv/gps/scigirls.html

Girlstart is an organization that aims to help girls succeed in math, science, and technology. There are a variety of afterschool programs and camps that this organization will help you develop. http://www.girlstart.org/index.asp

Sally Ride Science Camps for Girls provide opportunities for girls to explore science, technology, and engineering. http://www.educationunlimited.com/sallyride/science.html

Sisters in Science is a program that has several different approaches to increasing girls' access to science and math programs. http://www.sistersinscience.org/

Techbridge is a program sponsored by the Chabot Space and Science Center in Oakland, CA, designed to encourage girls in technology, engineering, and science. There is information on the site to help others start a girls' technology/science program. http://www.techbridgegirls.org/

The Lake Tahoe Watershed Project was a project where very capable middle-school girls worked together with female scientists in a camp atmosphere on ecological activities (Rohrer & Welsch, 1998). Reports of the project may give you ideas for developing a similar project of your own.

The National Education Association Web site has a section devoted to math and science programs for girls. http://www.nea.org/webresources/mathsciencegirlslinks.html

The National Science Foundation has an afterschool program called *Great Science for Girls.* http://www.afterschool.org/sga/gsg.cfm.

The *Science Club* has programs to increase science literacy for girls from underserved populations. These programs are free, after school, and provide opportunities for experiential learning, mentorship, and leadership. http://www.scienceclubforgirls.org

A long list of programs associated with colleges and universities can be found at http://www.academic.org/programs.html. These are just a few of the programs available to encourage the interests of girls in science.

Web Sites With Good Materials for Math and Science

There are many sources for this sort of information, and this list is certainly not exhaustive, but these sources I have found useful and reliable. The list is in alphabetic order and is not listed in any order of significance.

http://www.apples4theteacher.com/math.html

http://www2.carolina.com

http://www.educationalinsights.com/cat_math.html

http://www.enasco.com/

http://www.fatbraintoys.com/index.cfm

http://www.firstinmath.com/visitor.asp

http://www.freyscientific.com/

http://www.hallbar.com/sciencekits.html

http://www.home4schoolgear.com/index.html

http://www.klikkomath.com/index.html

http://www.lego.com/education/

http://www.naturesodyssey.com/

http://www.sciencekit.com

http://www.scientificsonline.com

http://www.skelementary.com

http://www.ucar.edu/sciencestore/index.htm

http://www.mindwareonline.com

LEARNING STYLE ASSESSMENTS

One of the problems teaching girls is finding out what their learning strengths are. What follows are two versions of an assessment that you can use to design study strategies for your students.

LEARNING STYLES PREFERENCE INVENTORY: ELEMENTARY LEVEL

This version is for teachers to take for young students.

How do your students process information? Does their learning style match your teaching style? By completing the inventory below for each of your students, you will gain greater insight into their preferred learning modalities. This knowledge can help you differentiate instruction and meet your students' needs.

Read each statement and select the appropriate number response as it applies to the student.

Often (3)   Sometimes (2)   Seldom/Never (1)

Visual Modality

_____ The child remembers information better if she can look at it (handouts, flashcards).

_____ The child stares intently at the teacher when the teacher is talking.

_____ The child seeks out a quiet place to work or turns her back to the class to work.

_____ The child can remember where information is on a page, but can't remember what the page says.

_____ The child does not remember directions given verbally, directions need to be written down or seen.

_____ The child remembers signs and landmarks when telling how to go somewhere.

_____ The child does not always understand jokes or mixes up words that look the same (*like* and *bike*).

_____ The child doodles and draws pictures on her work.

_____ The child pays close attention when the teacher is talking, but she has a hard time remembering what the teacher says, even though she remembers what the teacher did.

_____ The child color-codes her work, frequently uses colored markers, or shows use of color in her work.

_____ *Total*

(Continued)

(Continued)

Auditory Modality

_____ The child has messy papers, and her backpack is cluttered and unorganized.

_____ The child reads with her index finger to track her place on the line.

_____ The child does not follow directions written on a page well.

_____ The child can remember directions if the teacher says them.

_____ The child has difficulty writing and would rather tell a story than write it.

_____ The child often mixes up homonyms because they sound the same (*hear* and *here*).

_____ The child likes to be read to rather than read for herself.

_____ The child quickly understands verbal emotional cues; for example, she knows that someone is angry by the individual's tone of voice.

_____ The child has a hard time reading smaller print and prefers to read larger print, even though her vision is fine.

_____ The child rubs her eyes often or squints when she reads, even though her vision is fine.

_____ *Total*

Kinesthetic Modality

_____ The child starts to work before she has read the directions or has heard the directions.

_____ The child has a hard time sitting at her desk for a long time—cannot last as long as the others.

_____ The child does best if she watches someone do something before she tries it for herself.

_____ The child solves problems by trial and error and will try one solution method many times before she changes this approach.

_____ The child may wiggle around a lot while reading and, if on the floor, will change positions frequently.

_____ The child takes breaks frequently from what she is doing and may do something else, such as visiting another child for a short while before returning to the task.

_____ The child has a hard time explaining how to do something step-by-step, may not keep the logical order when telling the steps.

_____ The child may be good at sports and, probably, likes several different types of sports.

_____The child uses her hands a lot when describing something.

_____ The child can learn by writing something several times or drawing a picture.

_____ *Total*

Verbal Modality

_____ The child reads a great deal.

_____ The child has a good vocabulary and easily picks up words from what she reads.

_____ The child would rather write a story than tell about it.

_____ The child can work at one task for a longer time than most, particularly if it involves reading.

_____ The child has a hard time answering questions and has difficulty sorting out what part of the information answers the question and what is off topic.

_____ The child likes to read out loud.

_____ The child is well organized, rarely loses her papers, and can find papers easily.

_____ The child may find that math is difficult because she does not understand what she is asked to do and may have trouble understanding the symbols.

_____ The child may get distracted when others are talking or when there are other lessons going on in the classroom.

_____The child likes handouts and keeps them all.

_____ *Total*

Total the score for each section. A score of 21 points or more in a modality indicates strength in that area. The highest of the four sections signifies the most efficient method of information intake. The second highest score indicates the modality that boosts the primary strength.

Note: This inventory is not meant to substitute for assessment designed to identify learning or other disabilities. Such disabilities must also be considered when designing a student's instruction. For example, a child with verbal processing strengths may still be unorganized and easily lose her papers because of other difficulties.

SOURCE: Howard & James, 2003, pp. 75–77.

LEARNING STYLES PREFERENCE INVENTORY: SECONDARY LEVEL

How do you process information? Does your learning style match the way your teacher is presenting the material? This inventory will help you gain insight into your preferred learning modality, which will help you select learning strategies for individual courses.

Read each statement and select the appropriate number response as it applies to you.

Often (3)   Sometimes (2)   Seldom/Never (1)

Visual Modality

_____ You remember information better if you can look at it (handouts, flashcards).

_____ You need to look at the teacher when the teacher is talking.

_____ You need to study in a quiet place, and it helps to turn your back to the class to work.

_____ You can remember where information is on a page, but you can't remember what the page says.

_____ You do not remember when you are told directions; you need directions to be written down.

_____You remember signs and landmarks when you give directions.

_____ You have a hard time understanding jokes and may mix up words that look the same (_like_ and _bike_).

_____ You doodle and draw pictures on your work.

_____ You pay close attention to what the teacher says, but you have a hard time remembering what the teacher said, even though you remember what the teacher did.

_____ You use different colored highlighters or use color to sort or code your work.

_____ _Total_

Auditory Modality

_____ You have a messy and cluttered backpack and desk, and your papers tend to be messy.

_____ When you read, it helps to use your index finger to track your place on the line.

_____ You have more trouble following written directions.

_____ You can remember directions better if the teacher says them.

_____ You have trouble writing, and it is easier for you to tell a story or give oral reports.

_____ You mix up homonyms because they sound the same (*hear* and *here*).

_____ You like to be read to rather than read for yourself.

_____ You can easily tell when someone is upset or excited by the way their voice sounds.

_____ You have a hard time reading small print and like larger print, even though your vision is fine.

_____ You rub your eyes often or squint when you read, even though you do not need glasses.

_____ *Total*

Kinesthetic Modality

_____ You often begin work before you read the directions or before the teacher finishes reading the directions.

_____ You have a hard time sitting at your desk for a long time.

_____ You prefer to watch someone do something before you try something new, rather than reading or hearing the directions.

_____ You like to try to figure problems out for yourself and may have a hard time changing the way you solve problems.

_____ You have a hard time sitting still while you are reading and may prefer to read on the floor.

_____ You prefer to take frequent breaks and like to change tasks often to stay focused.

_____ You have a hard time explaining the steps of how to do something and may get the steps out of order.

_____ You may like sports and are probably good at several different types of sports.

_____ You use your hands a lot when you are describing something.

_____ You can learn by writing something down several times or drawing a picture or chart.

_____ *Total*

(Continued)

(Continued)

Verbal Modality

_____ You read a great deal.

_____ You have a good vocabulary and easily pick up words from the context.

_____ You would rather write a story than tell about it.

_____ You can work at one task longer than most other people, particularly if reading is involved.

_____ You may have a hard time answering questions because you include too much information and have difficulty sorting out what is important and what is not.

_____ You like to read out loud.

_____ You are well organized, rarely lose papers, and can find your schoolwork easily.

_____ You may find math difficult because you have trouble with what the question asks you to do and are not always sure of what the symbols mean.

_____ You may get distracted when others are talking or when there are other lessons going on in the classroom.

_____ You keep all the papers that you get from your teacher.

_____ *Total*

Total the score for each section. A score of 21 points or more in a modality indicates strength in that area. The highest of four sections signifies the most efficient way for you to access information. The second highest score indicates the modality that boosts your primary strength.

Another way to discover ways to assist students whose learning approaches may not fit the rest of your class is to use the multiple intelligences paradigm.

SOURCE: Adapted from Howard & James, 2003, p. 75–77

References

Ackerman, P. L., Bowen, K. R., Beier, M. E., & Kanfer, R. (2001). Determinants of individual differences and gender differences in knowledge. *Journal of Educational Psychology, 93*(4), 797–825.

Altermatt, E. R., & Kim, M. E. (2004). Can anxiety explain sex differences in college entrance exam scores? *Journal of College Admission, 183*, 6–11.

American Association of University Women (AAUW). (1992). *How schools short-change girls: The AAUW report.* New York: Marlowe & Company.

American Association of University Women (AAUW). (2008). *AAUW's position on science, technology, engineering, and mathematics (stem) education.* Retrieved March 13, 2008, from http://www.aauw.org/advocacy/issue_advocacy/actionpages/STEM.cfm.

Andre, T., Whigham, M., Hendrickson, A., & Chambers, S. (1999). Competency beliefs, positive affect, and gender stereotypes of elementary students and their parents about science versus other school subjects. *Journal of Research in Science Teaching, 36*(6), 719–747.

Anno, M., & Anno, M. (1983). *Anno's mysterious multiplying jar.* New York: Philomel Books.

Apter, T. (2006). Resolving the confidence crisis. *Educational Leadership, 63*(7), 42–46.

Armstrong, T. (1996). ADD: Does it really exist? *Phi Delta Kappan, 77*(6), 424–428.

Barnett, M. A., Quackenbush, S. W., & Sinisi, C. (1996). Factors affecting children's, adolescents', and young adults' perceptions of parental discipline. *Journal of Genetic Psychology, 157*(4), 411–424.

Baron-Cohen, S. (2003). *The essential difference: The truth about the male and female brain.* New York: Basic Books.

Beller, M., & Gafni, N. (1996). The 1991 international assessment of educational progress in mathematics and sciences: The gender differences perspective. *Journal of Educational Psychology, 88*(2), 365–377.

Benenson, J., & Christakos, A. (2003). The greater fragility of females' versus males' closest same-sex friendship. *Child Development, 74*(4), 1123–1129.

Benenson, J. F., & Heath, A. (2006). Boys withdraw more in one-on-one inter-actions, whereas girls withdraw more in groups. *Developmental Psychology, 42*(2), 272–282.

Beshir, M. Y., & Ramsey, J. D. (1981). Comparison between male and female subjective estimates of thermal effects and sensations. *Applied Ergonomics, 12*(1), 29–33.

Bleeker, M. M., & Jacobs, J. E. (2004). Achievement in math and science: Do mothers' beliefs matter 12 years later? *Journal of Educational Psychology, 96*(1), 97–109.

Blickenstaff, J. C. (2005). Women and science careers: Leaky pipeline or gender filter? *Gender and Education, 17*(4), 369–386.

Boyatzis, C. J., Chazan, E., & Ting, C. Z. (1993). Preschool children's decoding of facial emotions. *Journal of Genetic Psychology, 154*(3), 375–382.

Breakwell, G., Vignoles, V. L., & Robertson, T. (2003). Stereotypes and crossed-category evaluations: The case of gender and science education. *British Journal of Psychology, 94*(4), 437–455.

Breland, H. M., Danos, D. O., Kahn, H. D., Kubota, M. Y., & Bonner, M. W. (1994). Performance versus objective testing and gender: An exploratory study of an advanced placement history examination. *Journal of Educational Measurement, 31*(4), 275–293.

Buck, G., & Ehlers, N. (2002). Four criteria for engaging girls in the middle level classroom. *Middle School Journal, 34*(1), 48–53.

Burkam, D. T., Lee, V. E., & Smerdon, B. A. (1997). Gender and science learning early in high school: Subject matter and laboratory experiences. *American Educational Research Journal, 34*(2), 297–331.

Burns, M. (1994). *The greedy triangle.* New York: Scholastic.

Cahill, L. (2003). Sex- and hemisphere-related influences on the neurobiology of emotionally influenced memory. *Progress in Neuro-Psychopharmacology & Biological Psychiatry, 27,* 1235–1241.

Carr, M., & Davis, H. (2001). Gender differences in arithmetic strategy use: A function of skill and preference. *Contemporary Educational Psychology, 26*(3), 330–347.

Carr, M., & Jessup, D. L. (1997). Gender differences in first-grade mathematics strategy use: Social and metacognitive influences. *Journal of Educational Psychology, 89*(2), 318–328.

Carreker, S. (2004). *Dyslexia: Beyond the myth.* Retrieved April 25, 2007, from http://www.ldonline.org/article/277.

Casey, M. B., Nuttall, R. L., & Pezaris, E. (2001). Spatial-mechanical reasoning skills versus mathematics self-confidence as mediators of gender differences on mathematics subtests using cross-national gender-based items. *Journal for Research in Mathematics, 32*(1), 28–57.

Casey, M. B., Nuttall, R. L., Pezaris, E., & Benbow, C. P. (1995). The influence of spatial ability on gender differences in mathematics college entrance test scores across diverse samples. *Developmental Psychology, 31*(4), 697–705.

Cassidy, J. W., & Ditty, K. M. (2001). Gender differences among newborns on a transient otoacoustic emissions test for hearing. *Journal of Music Therapy, 38*(1), 28–35.

Cattaneo, Z., Postma, A., & Vecchi, T. (2006). Gender differences in memory for object and word locations. *Quarterly Journal of Experimental Psychology, 59*(5), 904–919.

Centers for Disease Control and Prevention. (2008, June 8). *Youth Risk Behavior Surveillance–United States, 2007.* Retrieved from http://www.cdc.gov/Healthy Youth/yrbs/pdf/yrbss07_mmwr.pdf.

Coleman, M. S. (2000). Undercounted and underpaid heroines: The path to equal opportunity in employment during the twentieth century. *Working USA, 3*(5), 37–65.

College Board (2006). 2006 college-bound seniors: Total group profile report. Retrieved from http://www.collegeboard.com/prod_downloads/about/news_info/cbsenior/yr2006/national-report.pdf.

Connellan, J., Baron-Cohen, S., Wheelwright, S., Batki, A., & Ahluwalia, J. (2000). Sex differences in human neonatal social perception. *Infant Behavior & Development, 23*(1), 113–118.

Corbett, C., Hill, C., & St. Rose, A. (2008). *Where the girls are: The facts about gender equity in education.* Washington, DC: American Association of University Women.

Corso, J. F. (1959). Age and sex differences in pure-tone thresholds. *The Journal of the Acoustical Society of America, 31*(4), 498–508.

Cox, A., & Fisher, M. (2008). A qualitative investigation of an all-female group in a software engineering course project. *Journal of Information Technology Education, 7*, 1–20.

Crowley, K., Callanan, M. A., Tenenbaum, H. R., & Allen, E. (2001). Parents explain more often to boys than to girls during shared scientific thinking. *Psychological Science, 12*(3), 258–261.

De Bellis, M. D., Keshavan, M. S., Beers, S. R., Hall, J., Frustaci, K., Masalehdan, A., et al. (2001). Sex differences in brain maturation during childhood and adolescence. *Cerebral Cortex, 11*, 552–557.

de Courten-Myers, G. M. (1999). The human cerebral cortex: Gender differences in structure and function. *Journal of Neuropathology and Experimental Neurology, 58*(3), 217–226.

de Goede, M., Kessels, R. P. C., & Postma, A. (2006). Individual variation in human spatial ability: Differences between men and women in object location memory. *Cognitive Processing, 7*(Suppl. 1), 153.

Dickhäuser, O., & Meyer, W. U. (2006). Gender differences in young children's math ability attributions. *Psychology Science, 48*(1), 3–16.

Ding, C. S., Song, K., & Richardson, L. I. (2006). Do mathematical gender differences continue? A longitudinal study of gender difference and excellence in mathematics performance in the U.S. *Journal of the American Educational Studies Association, 40*(3), 279–295.

Ding, N., & Harskamp, E. (2006). How partner gender influences female students' problem solving in physics education. *Journal of Science Education and Technology, 15*(5), 331–343.

Dresel, M., Ziegler, A., Broome, P., & Heller, K. A. (1998). Gender differences in science education: The double-edged role of prior knowledge in physics. *Roeper Review, 21*(2), 101–106.

Du, Y., Weymouth, C. M., & Dragseth, K. (2003, April 21–25). *Gender differences and student learning.* Paper presented at the annual meeting of the American Educational Research Association, Chicago, IL.

Duckworth, A. L., & Seligman, M. E. P. (2006). Self-discipline gives girls the edge: Gender in self-discipline, grades, and achievement test scores. *Journal of Educational Psychology, 98*(1), 198–208.

Dysgraphia. (2007). Retrieved April 25, 2007, from http://www.ncld.org/index.php?option=content&task=view&id=468.

Elliott, C. D. (1971). Noise tolerance and extraversion in children. *British Journal of Psychology, 62*(3), 375–380.

Epstein, D. (1999). Real boys don't work: "Underachievement," masculinity, and the harassment of "sissies." In D. Epstein, J. Elwood, V. Hey, & J. Maw (Eds.), *Failing boys? Issues in gender and achievement.* Philadelphia, PA: Open University Press.

Feist, G. J. (2006). How development and personality influence scientific thought, interest, and achievement. *Review of General Psychology, 10*(2), 163–182.

Fennema, E., Carpenter, T. P., Jacobs, V. R., Franke, M., & Levi, L. W. (1998). A longitudinal study of gender differences in young children's mathematical thinking. *Educational Researcher, 27*(5), 6–11.

Fennema, E., Peterson, P. L., Carpenter, T. P., & Lubinski, C. A. (1990). Teachers' attributions and beliefs about girls, boys, and mathematics. *Educational Studies in Mathematics, 21*(1), 55–69.

Ferreira, M. (2001). Building communities through role models, mentors, and hands-on-science. *School Community Journal, 11*(2), 27–37.

Fine, J. G., Semrud-Clikeman, M., Keith, T., Stapleton, L. M., & Hynd, G. W. (2007). Reading and the corpus callosum: An MRI family study of volume and area. *Neuropsychology, 21*(2), 235–241.

Forgasz, H. J., Leder, G. C., & Kloosterman, P. (2004). New perspectives on the gender stereotyping of mathematics. *Mathematical Thinking and Learning, 6*(4), 389–420.

Frenzel, A. C., Pekrun, R., & Goetz, T. (2007). Girls and mathematics—A "hopeless" issue? A control-value approach to gender differences in emotions towards mathematics. *European Journal of Psychology of Education, 22*(4), 497–514.

Friedman, L. (1995). The space factor in mathematics: Gender differences. *Review of Educational Research, 65*(1), 22–50.

Frings, L., Wagner, K., Uterrainer, J., Spreer, J., Halsband, U., & Schulze-Bonhage, A. (2006). Gender-related differences in lateralization of hippocampal activation and cognitive strategy. *NeuroReport, 17*(4), 417–421.

Gallagher, A. M. (1998). Gender and antecedents of performance in mathematics testing. *Teachers College Record, 100*(2), 297–314.

Gallagher, A. M., & De Lisi, R. (1994). Gender differences in scholastic aptitude test-mathematics problem solving among high-ability students. *Journal of Educational Psychology, 86*(2), 204–211.

Gallagher, A. M., & Kaufman, J. C. (2005). Gender differences in mathematics. In A. M. Gallagher & J. C. Kaufman (Eds.), *Gender difference in mathematics: An integrative psychological approach.* New York: Cambridge University Press.

Gardner, H. (1983). *Frames of mind: The theory of multiple intelligences.* New York: Basic Books.

Gaub, M., & Carlson, C. (1997). Gender differences in ADHD: A meta-analysis and critical review. *Journal of the American Academy of Child and Adolescent Psychiatry, 36*(8), 1036–1045.

Geffen, G., Moar, K. J., Hanlon, A. P., Clark, C. R., & Geffen, L. B. (1990). Performance measures of 16- to 86-year-old males and females on the auditory verbal learning test. *Clinical Neuropsychologist, 4*(1), 45–63.

Geiger, J. F., & Litwiller, R. M. (2005). Spatial working memory and gender differences in science. *Journal of Instructional Psychology, 32*(1), 49–57.

Giedd, J. N., Blumenthal, J., Jeffries, N. O., Castellanos, F. X., Liu, H., Zijdenbos, A., et al. (1999). Brain development during childhood and adolescence: A longitudinal MRI study. *Nature Neuroscience, 2*(10), 861–863.

Giedd, J. N., Blumenthal, J. D., Jeffries, N. O., Rajapakse, J. C., Vaituzis, A. C., Liu, H., et al. (1999). Development of the human corpus callosum during childhood and adolescence: A longitudinal MRI study. *Progress in Neuro-Psychopharmacology & Biological Psychiatry, 23,* 571–588.

Giedd, J. N., Castellanos, F. X., Rajapakse, J. C., Vaituzis, A. C., & Raporport, J. L. (1997). Sexual dimorphism of the developing human brain. *Progress in Neuro-Psychopharmacology & Biological Psychiatry, 21,* 1185–1201.

Gould, J. C., Weeks, V., & Evans, S. (2003). Science starts early. *Gifted Child Today, 26*(2), 38–42.

Green, K. S., & Gynther, M. D. (1995). Blue versus periwinkle: Color identification and gender. *Perceptual and Motor Skills, 80*(1), 27–32.

Guiso, L., Monte, F., Sapienza, P., & Zingales, L. (2008, May 30). Culture, gender, and math. *Science, 320,* 1164–1165.

Gur, R., Alsop, D., Glahn, D., Petty, R., Swanson, C. L., Maldjian, J. A., et al. (2000). An fMRI study of sex differences in regional activation to a verbal and a spatial task. *Brain and Language, 74,* 157–170.

Guzzetti, B. J. (2001). Texts and talk: The role of gender in learning physics. In E. B. Moje & D. G. O'Brien (Eds.), *Constructions of literacy: Studies of teaching and learning in and out of secondary schools.* Mahwah, NJ: Lawrence Erlbaum.

Halpern, D. F. (2000). *Sex differences in cognitive abilities* (3rd ed.). Mahwah, NJ: Lawrence Erlbaum.

Halpern, D. F., Benbow, C. P., Geary, D. C., Gur, R. C., Shibley Hyde, J., & Gernsbacher, M. A. (2007). The science of sex differences in science and mathematics. *Psychological Science in the Public Interest, 8*(1), 1–51.

Hammrich, P. L. (1998). Sisters in science: An intergenerational science program for elementary school girls. *School Community Journal, 8*(2), 21–35.

Harshman, R. A., & Paivio, A. (1987). "Paradoxical" sex differences in self-reported imagery. *Canadian Journal of Psychology, 41*(3), 287–302.

Heacox, D. (2002). *Differentiating instruction in the regular classroom: How to reach and teach all learners, grades 3–12.* Minneapolis, MN: Free Spirit.

Henrie, R. L., Aron, R. H., Nelson, B., & Poole, D. A. (1997). Gender-related knowledge variations within geography. *Sex Roles, 36*(9–10), 605–623.

Herbert, J., & Stipek, D. (2005). The emergence of gender differences in children's perceptions of their academic competence. *Applied Developmental Psychology, 26,* 276–296.

Hinshaw, S. P., Owens, E. B., Sami, N., & Fargeon, S. (2006). Prospective follow-up of girls with attention-deficit/hyperactivity disorder into adolescence: Evidence for continuing cross-domain impairment. *Journal of Consulting and Clinical Psychology, 74*(3), 489–499.

Hirt, E. R., McCrea, S. M., & Boris, H. I. (2003). "I know you self-handicapped last exam": Gender differences in reactions to self-handicapping. *Journal of Personality and Social Psychology, 84*(1), 177–193.

Hodgson, B. (2000). Women in science—or are they? *Physics Education, 35*(6), 451–453.

Hoffman, L. (2002). Promoting girls' interest and achievement in physics classes for beginners. *Learning and Instruction, 12,* 447–465.

Hong, E., O'Neil, H. F., & Feldon, D. (2005). Gender effects on mathematics achievement. In A. M. Gallagher & J. C. Kaufman (Eds.), *Gender differences in mathematics: An integrative psychological approach.* New York: Cambridge University Press.

Honigsfeld, A., & Dunn, R. (2003). High school male and female learning-style similarities and differences in diverse nations. *The Journal of Educational Research, 96*(4), 195–207.

Horton, N. K., Ray, G. E., & Cohen, R. (2001). Children's evaluations of inductive discipline as a function of transgression type and induction orientation. *Child Study Journal, 31*(2), 71–93.

Howard, L., & James, A. N. (2003). *What principals need to know about teaching: Differentiated instruction.* Alexandria, VA: National Association of Elementary School Principals.

Huang, J. (1993). An investigation of gender differences in cognitive abilities among Chinese high school students. *Personality and Individual Differences, 15*(6), 717–719.

Huguet, P., & Régner, I. (2007). Stereotype threat among schoolgirls in quasi-ordinary classroom circumstances. *Journal of Educational Psychology, 99*(3), 545–560.

Hunt, D. M. (2007). *The 2007 Hollywood writers report: Whose stories are we telling?* Los Angeles, CA: Writers Guild of America, West.

Huttenlocher, J., Haight, W., Bryk, A., Seltzer, M., & Lyons, T. (1991). Early vocabulary growth: Relation to language input and gender. *Developmental Psychology, 27*(2), 236–248.

Hyde, J. S. (2005). The gender similarities hypothesis. *American Psychologist, 60*(6), 581–592.

Hyde, J. S., Fennema, E., & Ryan, M. (1990). Gender comparisons of mathematics attitudes and affect. *Psychology of Women Quarterly, 14*(3), 299–324.

Iijima, M., Arisaka, O., Minamoto, F., & Arai, Y. (2001). Sex differences in children's free drawings: A study on girls with congenital adrenal hyperplasia. *Hormones and Behavior, 40*(2), 99–104.

Jackson, T., Iezzi, T., Gunderson, J., Nagasaka, T., & Fritch, A. (2002). Gender differences in pain perception: The mediating role of self-efficacy. *Sex Roles, 47*(11), 561–568.

Jacobs, J. E., & Bleeker, M. M. (2004). Girls' and boys' developing interests in math and science: Do parents matter? *New Directions for Child and Adolescent Development, 106*, 5–21.

James, A. N. (2007). *Teaching the male brain: How boys think, feel, and learn in school.* Thousand Oaks, CA: Corwin.

Jenkins, E. W., & Nelson, N. W. (2005). Important but not for me: Students' attitudes towards secondary school science in England. *Research in Science and Technological Education, 23*(1), 41–57.

Johns, M., Schmader, T., & Martens, A. (2005). Knowing is half the battle: Teaching stereotype threat as a means of improving women's math performance. *Psychological Science, 16*(3), 175–179.

Johnson, E. S., & Meade, A. C. (1987). Developmental patterns of spatial ability: An early sex difference. *Child Development, 58*, 725–740.

Jonassen, D. H., & Grabowski, B. L. (1993). *Handbook of individual differences, learning, and instruction.* Hillsdale, NJ: Lawrence Erlbaum.

Jones, L. G. (1989). Context, confidence and the able girl. *Educational Research, 31*(3), 189–194.

Jones, M. G., Brader-Araje, L., Carboni, L. W., Carter, G., Rua, M. J., Banilower, E., et al. (2000). Tool time: Gender and students' use of tools, control, and authority. *Journal of Research in Science Teaching, 37*(8), 760–783.

Kahle, J. B. (1989). *Images of scientists: Gender issues in science classrooms.* Perth, Australia: Curtin University of Technology.

Kalist, D. E. (2002). The gender earnings gap in the RN labor market. *Nursing Economics, 20*(4), 155–162.

Kaufmann, L., Lochy, A., Drexler, A., & Semenza, C. (2004). Deficient arithmetic fact retrieval—storage or access problem? *Neuropsychologia, 42*(4), 482–496.

Keller, C. (2001). Effect of teachers' stereotyping on students' stereotyping of mathematics as a male domain. *The Journal of Social Psychology, 14*(2), 165–173.

Keller, J. (2002). Blatant stereotype threat and women's math performance: Self-handicapping as a strategic means to cope with obtrusive negative performance expectations. *Sex Roles, 47*(3/4), 193–198.

Kennedy, H. L., & Parks, J. (2000). Society cannot continue to exclude women from the fields of science and mathematics. *Education, 120*(3), 529–537.

Kenney-Benson, G. A., Pomerantz, E. M., Ryan, A. M., & Patrick, H. (2006). Sex differences in math performance: The role of children's approach to schoolwork. *Developmental Psychology, 42*(1), 11–26.

Keri, G. (2002). Male and female college students' learning styles differ: An opportunity for instructional diversification. *College Student Journal, 36*(3), 433–441.

Killgore, W. D. S., Oki, M., & Yurgelun-Todd, D. A. (2001). Sex-specific developmental changes in amygdala responses to affective faces. *NeuroReport, 12*(2), 427–433.

Kimball, M. M. (1989). A new perspective on women's math achievement. *Psychological Bulletin, 105*(2), 198–214.

Kimura, D. (2000). *Sex and cognition.* Cambridge, MA: A Bradford Book/The MIT Press.

Kozhevnikov, M., Kosslyn, S., & Shephard, J. (2005). Spatial versus object visualizers: A new characterization of visual cognitive style. *Memory & Cognition, 33*(4), 710–726.

Kramer, J. H., Delis, D. C., Kaplan, E., O'Donnell, L., & Prifitera, A. (1997). Developmental sex differences in verbal learning. *Neuropsychology, 11*(4), 577–584.

Lachance, J. A., & Mazzocco, M. M. M. (2006). A longitudinal analysis of sex differences in math and spatial skills in primary school age children. *Learning & Individual Differences, 16*(3), 195–216.

Lawton, C. A., & Hatcher, D. W. (2005). Gender differences in integration of images in visuospatial memory. *Sex Roles, 53*(9–10), 717–725.

Lazear, D. (1992). *Teaching for multiple intelligences.* Bloomington, IN: Phi Delta Kappa Educational Foundation.

Lesko, A. C., & Corpus, J. H. (2006). Discounting the difficult: How high math-identified women respond to stereotype threat. *Sex Roles, 54*(1–2), 113–125.

Lewin, C., Wolgers, G., & Herlitz, A. (2001). Sex differences favoring women in verbal but not visuospatial episodic memory. *Neuropsychology, 15*(2), 165–173.

Linderman, J., Kantrowitz, L., & Flannery, K. (2005). Male vulnerability to reading disability is not likely to be a myth: A call for new data. *Journal of Learning Disabilities, 38*(2), 109–129.

Linn, M., & Petersen, A. (1985). Emergence and characterization of sex differences in spatial ability. *Child Development, 56*, 1479–1498.

Lippa, R. (1998). Gender-related individual differences and the structure of vocational interests: The importance of the people-things dimension. *Journal of Personality and Social Psychology, 74*(4), 996–1009.

Lloyd, J. E. V., Walsh, J., & Yailagh, M. S. (2005). Sex differences in performance attributions, self-efficacy, and achievement in mathematics: If I'm so smart, why don't I know it? *Canadian Journal of Education, 28*(3), 384–408.

Logan, K. (2007). Should computing be taught in single-sex environments? An analysis of the computing learning environment of upper secondary students. *Educational Studies, 33*(2), 233–248.

Longcamp, M., Boucard, C., Gilhodes, J. C., Anton, J. L., Roth, M., Nazarian, B., et al. (2008). Learning through hand- or typewriting influences visual recognition of new graphic shapes: Behavioral and functional imaging evidence. *Journal of Cognitive Neuroscience, 20*(5), 802–815.

Longcamp, M., Boucard, C., Gilhodes, J. C., & Velay, J. L. (2006). Remembering the orientation of newly learned characters depends on the associated writing knowledge: A comparison between handwriting and typing. *Human Movement Science, 25*, 646–656.

Lubinski, D., Webb, R. M., Morelock, M. J., & Benbow, C. P. (2001). Top 1 in 10,000: A 10-year follow-up of the profoundly gifted. *Journal of Applied Psychology, 86*(4), 718–729

Lucas, J. W., & Lovaglia, M. J. (2005). Self-handicapping: Gender, race, and status. *Current Research in Social Psychology, 10*(15), 234–249.

Lummis, M., & Stevenson, H. W. (1990). Gender differences in beliefs and achievement: A cross-cultural study. *Developmental Psychology, 26*(2), 254–263.

Lutchmaya, S., & Baron-Cohen, S. (2002). Human sex differences in social and non-social looking preferences, at 12 months of age. *Infant Behavior & Development, 25*(3), 319–325.

Lynn, R., & Irwing, P. (2002). Sex differences in general knowledge, semantic memory, and reasoning ability. *British Journal of Psychology, 93*(4), 545–556.

Maccoby, E. E. (1998). *The two sexes: Growing up apart, growing together.* Cambridge, MA: Harvard University Press.

Majeres, R. L. (1999). Sex differences in phonological processes: Speeded matching and word reading. *Memory & Cognition, 27*(2), 246–253.

Martins, I. P., Castro-Caldas, A., Townes, B. D., Ferreira, G., Rodrigues, P., Marques, S., et al. (2005). Age and sex differences in neurobehavioral performance: A study of Portuguese elementary school children. *International Journal of Neuroscience, 115*, 1687–1709.

McClure, E. B. (2000). A meta-analytic review of sex differences in facial expression processing and their development in infants, children, and adolescents. *Psychological Bulletin, 126*(3), 424–453.

McEwen, A., Knipe, D., & Gallagher, T. (1997). The impact of single-sex and coeducational schooling on participation and achievement in science: A 10-year perspective. *Research in Science and Technological Education, 15*(2), 223–233.

McFadden, D. (1998). Sex differences in the auditory system. *Developmental Neuropsychology, 14*(2–3), 261–298.

McGuiness, D. (1976). Away from a unisex psychology: Individual differences in visual sensory and perceptual processes. *Perception, 5*(3), 279–294.

Meece, J. L., & Jones, M. G. (1996). Gender differences in motivation and strategy use in science: Are girls rote learners? *Journal of Research in Science Teaching, 33*(4), 393–406.

Miller, P. H., Blessing, J. S., & Schwartz, S. (2006). Gender differences in high-school students' views about science. *International Journal of Science Education, 28*(4), 363–381.

Miller, R. J. (2001). Gender differences in illusion response: The influence of spatial strategy and sex ratio. *Sex Roles, 44*(3–4), 209–225.

Morgan, C., Isaac, J. D., & Sansone, C. (2001). The role of interest in understanding the career choices of female and male college students. *Sex Roles, 44*(5–6), 295–318.

Morton, B. E., & Rafto, S. E. (2006). Corpus callosum size is linked to dichotic deafness and hemisphericity, not sex or handedness. *Brain and Cognition, 62*(1), 1–8.

Mulvey, P. J., & Nicholson, S. (2006). *Enrollments and degree reports, 2004.* College Park, MD: American Institute of Physics.

Naglieri, J. A., & Rojahn, J. (2001). Gender differences in planning, attention, simultaneous, and successive (pass) cognitive processes and achievement. *Journal of Educational Psychology, 93*(2), 430–437.

Naka, M. (1998). Repeated writing facilitates children's memory for pseudocharacters and foreign letters. *Memory and Cognition, 26*(4), 804–809.

National Center for Educational Statistics (NCES). (2007a). *Percentage of students from kindergarten through eighth grade participating in weekly nonparental after-school care arrangements: 2005.* Washington, DC: U.S. Department of Education.

National Center for Educational Statistics (NCES). (2007b). *The nation's report card: An introduction to the national assessment of educational progress (NAEP).* Washington, DC: U.S. Department of Education.

National Science Foundation, Division of Science Resources Statistics. (2007). *Women, minorities, and persons with disabilities in science and engineering,* (NSF 07–315). Arlington, VA: Author.

Neuschwander, C. (1997). *Sir cumference and the round table.* Waltertown, MA: Charlesbridge.

Njemanze, P. C. (2007). Cerebral lateralisation for facial processing: Gender-related cognitive styles determined using fourier analysis of mean cerebral blood flow velocity in the middle cerebral arteries. *Laterality, 12*(1), 31–49.

Papanicolaou, A. C., Simos, P. G., Castillo, E., Breier, J., Katz, J. S., & Wright, A. A. (2002). The hippocampus and memory of verbal and pictorial material. *Learning and Memory, 9*(3), 99–104.

Penner, A. M. (2003). International gender x item difficulty interactions in mathematics and science achievement tests. *Journal of Educational Psychology, 95*(3), 650–655.

Pomerantz, E. M., Altermatt, E. R., & Saxon, J. J. (2002). Making the grade, but feeling distressed: Gender differences in academic performance and internal distress. *Journal of Educational Psychology, 94*(2), 396–404.

Pomerantz, E. M., & Ruble, D. N. (1998). The role of maternal control in the development of sex differences in child self-evaluative factors. *Child Development, 69*(2), 458–478.

Posadas, B. M. (1997). Crossing the collar line: Working women at desks, switchboards, and tables. *Journal of Urban History, 23*(6), 777–788.

Pyryt, M. C., Sandals, L. H., & Begoray, J. (1998). Learning style preferences of gifted, average-ability, and special needs students: A multivariate perspective. *Journal for Research in Childhood Education, 13*(1), 71–76.

Quaiser-Pohl, C., & Lehmann, W. (2002). Girls' spatial abilities: Charting the contributions of experiences and attitudes in different academic groups. *British Journal of Educational Psychology, 72,* 245–260.

Räty, H., & Kasanen, K. (2007). Gendered views of ability in parents' perceptions of their children's academic competencies. *Sex Roles, 56,* 117–124.

Rahm, J., & Moore, J. C. (2005). The role of afterschool and community science programs in the lives of urban youth. *School Science and Mathematics, 105*(6), 383–391.

Reid, P. T., & Roberts, S. K. (2006). Gaining options: A mathematics program for potentially talented at-risk adolescent girls. *Merrill-Palmer Quarterly, 52*(2), 288–304.

Robert, M., & Harel, F. (1996). The gender difference in orienting liquid surfaces and plumb-lines: Its robustness, its correlates and the associated knowledge of physics. *Canadian Journal of Experimental Psychology, 50*(3), 280–314.

Rucklidge, J. J., & Tannock, R. (2001). Psychiatric, psychosocial, and cognitive functioning of female adolescents with ADHD. *Journal of the American Academy of Child and Adolescent Psychiatry, 40*(5), 530–540.

Salminen-Karlsson, M. (2007). Girls' groups and boys' groups at a municipal technology centre. *International Journal of Science Education, 29*(8), 1019–1033.

Sasser, A. C. (2005). Gender differences in physician pay. *The Journal of Human Resources, 40*(2), 476–504.

Sax, L. (2005). *Why gender matters.* New York: Doubleday.

Sax, L. (2008, June 18). Where the girls aren't. *Education Week, 27*(42), 36–29.

Seitsinger, A. M., Barboza, H. C., & Hird, A. (1998, April 13–17). *Single-sex mathematics instruction in an urban independent school.* Paper presented at the annual meeting of the American Educational Research Association, San Diego, CA.

Shalev, R. S. (2004). Developmental dyscalculia. *Journal of Child Neurology, 19*(10), 765–770.

Shaywitz, B., Shaywitz, S. E., Pugh, K. R., Constable, R. T., Skudlarski, P., Fulbright, R. K., et al. (1995). Sex differences in the functional organization of the brain for language. *Nature, 373,* 607–609.

Shettle, C., Roey, S., Mordica, J., Perkins, R., Nord, C., Teodorovic, J., et al. (2007). *The nation's report card: America's high school graduates.* In Department of Education (Ed.), (NCES 2007–467). Washington, DC: U.S. Government Printing Office.

Shucard, J. L., & Shucard, D. W. (1990). Auditory evoked potentials and hand preference in 6-month-old infants: Possible gender-related differences in cerebral organization. *Developmental Psychology, 26*(6), 923–930.

Snowden, R. J. (2002). Visual attention to color: Parvocellular guidance of attentional resources? *Psychological Science, 13*(2), 180–184.

Snyder, T. D., Tan, A. G., & Hoffman, C. M. (2006). *Digest of education statistics 2005.* In U.S. Department of Education (Ed.), (Vol. NCES 2006–030). Washington, DC: U.S. Government Printing Office.

Spelke, E. S. (2005). Sex differences in intrinsic aptitude for mathematics and science? *American Psychologist, 60*(9), 950–958.

Spencer, S. J., Steele, C. M., & Quinn, D. M. (1999). Stereotype threat and women's math performance. *Journal of Experimental Social Psychology, 35*(1), 4–28.

Spreen, O., & Strauss, E. (1998). *A compendium of neuropsychological tests: Administration, norms, and commentary.* New York: Oxford University Press.

Steele, J., James, J. B., & Barnett, R. C. (2002). Learning in a man's world: Examining the perceptions of undergraduate women in male-dominated academic areas. *Psychology of Women Quarterly, 26,* 46–50.

Stipek, D., & Gralinski, J. H. (1991). Gender differences in children's achievement-related beliefs and emotional responses to success and failure in mathematics. *Journal of Educational Psychology, 83*(3), 361–371.

Stumpf, H. (1998). Gender-related differences in academically talented students' scores and use of time on tests of spatial ability. *Gifted Child Quarterly, 42*(3), 157–171.

Taylor, S. E., Klein, L. C., Lewis, B. P., Gruenewald, T. L., Gurung, R. A. R., & Updegraff, J. A. (2000). Biobehavioral responses to stress in females: Tend-and-befriend, not fight-or-flight. *Psychological Review, 107*(3), 411–429.

Tenenbaum, H. R., & Leaper, C. (2003). Parent-child conversations about science: The socialization of gender inequities? *Developmental Psychology, 39*(1), 34–47.

Thies, A. P. (1999–2000). The neuropsychology of learning styles. *National Forum of Applied Educational Research Journal, 13*(1), 50–62.

Tibbetts, S. L. (1977). Sex-role stereotyping and its effects on boys. *Journal of the NAWDAC, 40*(3), 109–111.

Tolley, K. (2003). *The science education of American girls.* New York: RoutledgeFalmer.

Tomlinson, C. A. (2004a). *How to differentiate instruction in mixed-ability classrooms* (2nd ed.). Alexandria, VA: Association for Supervision and Curriculum Development.

Tomlinson, C. A. (2004b). *The differentiated classroom: Responding to the needs of all learners.* Upper Saddle River, NJ: Prentice Hall.

Trahan, D. E., & Quintana, J. W. (1990). Analysis of gender effects upon verbal and visual memory performance in adults. *Archives of Clinical Neuropsychology, 5*(4), 325–334.

Turton, S., & Campbell, C. (2005). Tend and befriend versus fight or flight: Gender differences in behavioral response to stress among university students. *Journal of Applied Biobehavioral Research, 10*(4), 209–232.

Tyack, D., & Hansot, E. (1990). *Learning together: A history of coeducation in American public schools.* New York: Yale University Press.

U.S. Bureau of Labor Statistics. (2006). *Women in the labor force: A databook.* Washington, DC: U.S. Government Printing Office.

U.S. Census Bureau. (2000). *Occupation by sex: 2000 qt–p27.* Washington, DC: U.S. Government Printing Office.

U.S. Census Bureau. (2006). *Statistical abstract of the United States: 2007* (126 ed.). Washington, DC: Government Printing Office.

U.S. Department of Education, National Center for Education Statistics. (2007). *Digest of education statistics.* Washington, DC: Government Printing Office.

Van Houtte, M. (2004). Why boys achieve less at school than girls: The difference between boys' and girls' academic culture. *Educational Studies, 30*(2), 159–173.

Velle, W. (1987). Sex differences in sensory functions. *Perspectives in Biology and Medicine, 30*(4), 490–522.

Vermeer, H. J., Boekaerts, M., & Seegers, G. (2000). Motivational and gender differences: Sixth-grade students' mathematical problem-solving behavior. *Journal of Educational Psychology, 92*(2), 308–315.

Virginia Department of Education. (2005). *Life science standards of learning.* Retrieved July 26, 2005, from http://www.doe.virginia.gov/go/Sols/science7.pdf.

Vuontela V., Steenari, M. R., Carlson, S., Koivisto, J., Fjallberg, M., & Aronen, E. T. (2003). Audiospatial and visuospatial working memory in 6–13 year old school children. *Learning and Memory, 10,* 74–81.

Warner, S., & Moore, S. (2004). Excuses, excuses: Self-handicapping in an Australian adolescent sample. *Journal of Youth and Adolescence, 33*(4), 271–281.

Webb, R. M., Lubinski, D., & Benbow, C. P. (2002). Mathematically facile adolescents with math-science aspirations: New perspectives on their educational and vocational development. *Journal of Educational Psychology, 94*(4), 785–794.

Wein, H. (2000). Stress and disease: New perspectives. *National Institute of Health Word on Health.* Retrieved from http://nces.ed.gov/program/digest/d04/tables/xls/tabnl21.xls.

Wigfield, A., & Meece, J. L. (1988). Math anxiety in elementary and secondary school students. *Journal of Educational Psychology, 80*(2), 210–216.

Wiggins, G., & McTighe, J. (2005). *Understanding by design* (2nd ed.). Alexandria, VA: Association for Supervision and Curriculum Development.

Witt, S. D. (1997). Parental influence on children's socialization to gender roles. *Adolescence, 32*(126), 253–259.

Yanowitz, K. L., & Vanderpool, S. S. (2004). Assessing girls' reactions to science workshops. *Journal of Science Education and Technology, 13*(3), 353–359.

Yurgelun-Todd, D. A., Killgore, W. D. S., & Cintron, C. B. (2003). Cognitive correlates of medial temporal lobe development across adolescence: A magnetic resonance imaging study. *Perceptual and Motor Skills, 96*(1), 3–17.

Zohar, A., & Sela, D. (2003). Her physics, his physics: Gender issues in Israeli advanced placement physics classes. *International Journal of Science Education, 25*(2), 245–268.

Index

CORWIN

A SAGE Company

The Corwin logo—a raven striding across an open book—represents the union of courage and learning. Corwin is committed to improving education for all learners by publishing books and other professional development resources for those serving the field of PreK–12 education. By providing practical, hands-on materials, Corwin continues to carry out the promise of its motto: **"Helping Educators Do Their Work Better."**